The GRACE MURDER Case

Written by
LISA MELVILLE

A SISU BOOKS Publication

The Grace Murder Case
Copyright © 2010 by Lisa Melville

All Rights Reserved. No Part of this book may be reproduced, in whole or part, without the express written consent of the author.

Titles from Sisu Books are available at quantity discounts for educational, business, or sales and promotional use. For information please visit us on the web at www.sisubooks.com for a complete list of titles available, or write to:

Sisu Books
PO Box 421
Sparrowbush, New York 12780

To contact the author: Melvillelisamarie@gmail.com

Cover design by Kimberly Easa.
Postcards used in the cover design are courtesy of Marcus Millspaugh

Notice: The information in this book is true and complete to the best of our knowledge. It is offered without guarantee on the part of the author or Sisu Books. The author and Sisu Books disclaim all liability in connection with the use of this book.

ISBN 13: 978-0-9842283-3-1
ISBN 10: 0-9842283-3-0

Published by Sisu Books, Sparrowbush, New York

For my sweet Adeline
and in memory of my grandfather, Frank Clement

TABLE OF CONTENTS

Acknowledgments ... vii

1
The Case ... 9

2
The Grace Brothers ... 37

3
The Trial ... 52

4
The Other Victims ... 85

5
The Execution ... 95

References ... 103

About the Author ... 105

ACKNOWLEDGEMENTS

This project took years to complete and there are so many people to thank. I want to express my gratitude to my parents, Ed and Lilli, for inspiring me and for always supporting me. I would like to thank my husband, Jim, for giving me time to research and for putting up with my passion for history. I am grateful to have a wonderful set of family and friends who have all in some way contributed to this work, whether it was a kind word or patiently listening to me as the story unfolded

I would like to thank Marcus Millspaugh for his help and for the use of his postcard and photograph collection. I would also like to express my appreciation to the Walden and Wallkill Valley Historical Society, the Minisink Valley Historical Society, the Ossining Historical Society, the City of Fall River Massachusetts Public Library, the Fall River Historical Society and especially Susan Fougstedt of the Pollard Memorial Library in Lowell Massachusetts.

1

THE CASE

"The most revolting and horrible [murder] ever committed in Orange County and it seems impossible that a brother could have done it, still suspicions point to him from every angle."[i] This is how George Ronk, Chief of the Walden Police Department, described the murder of Jack Grace. Jack's mutilated, decomposing body was found in the Twentieth Century Club rooms on Main Street in Walden, New York on September 11, 1912. He was only 28 years old. The primary suspect of his brutal murder was his brother, Antone William Grace, known in Walden as Bill Grace.

The Grace Brothers were from Fall River, Massachusetts where the famous "Lizzie Borden" murder case had occurred. Even if you have not heard of the actual Borden case, most people have heard of the famous children's playground verse: "Lizzie Borden took an axe and gave her mother forty whacks. And when she saw what she had done, she gave her father forty-one."

Lizzie Borden was accused of murdering her father and stepmother with a hatchet. Antone Grace was accused of killing his brother with a meat cleaver. The similarity in the murder weapons and of murdering family members is intriguing. The Grace murder was the "Lizzie Borden" case of Walden, New York. Murder was not a common occurrence in this small village, and this crime was a scandalous case that included sex, lies, and a violent crime. It rocked this small community. The "Lizzie Borden" case is still one of the most famous cases in the United States. While Lizzie's gender made her case sensational,

The Grace Murder Case

the Grace case possessed the same kind of startling characteristics. It involved fratricide and bigamy in a time when a woman's life was completely defined by whom she married. Bill Grace not only abandoned his first wife with three children, but this cad married a second woman, left her while she was pregnant with their child, and stole her family's money to make his escape. Bill used this money to help finance a new life for himself in Walden that included yet another wife. Despite the titillating facts of the murder, the Grace case has nearly been forgotten.

Lizzie Borden was found not guilty. Antone Grace was not so lucky. He was found guilty of first-degree murder in the death of his brother and was electrocuted at Sing Sing less than a year after the murder. His trial was completed in two days; the guilty verdict took less than an hour even though the case was based on circumstantial evidence. He was sentenced to death and filed an appeal. His appeal was unsuccessful and was over by March of 1913. Grace's court appointed lawyer was Wilton Bennet, from Port Jervis, New York. He did not seem to present a very strong case for Bill Grace, although he had made an impassioned and flowery appeal to the jury. "His remarks were very earnest and forceful but it was the opinion of lawyers present that any effect which they might have had upon the jury was utterly dispelled by the miserable showing made on the stand by Grace himself."[ii]

In his last attempt to save his life, Bill Grace made a plea for clemency to Governor Sultzer. It was denied. Governor Sultzer was the only New York State Governor to be impeached, and he was in the midst of that impeachment when Bill Grace made his request for clemency so he may have been somewhat preoccupied. Bill Grace was truly out of luck.

Born in Fall River, Massachusetts in 1887, Antone William Grace was five years old when the Lizzie Borden case took

The Case

place. His family lived on 548 Palmer Street, which was only about a mile away from 92 Second Street where the Borden murders took place. It is quite possible that he grew up hearing about the Lizzie Borden case and it may be what he drew from when he was thinking of how to murder someone. In fact, Lizzie Borden outlived Bill Grace by fourteen years and may have read about his crimes in the Fall River paper or the *New York Times*.

Antone William Grace and Jack Grace had come to Walden from Massachusetts sometime in late 1910. By most accounts, they were friendly with each other and spent a lot of time together. They were working class men and had become well known in the Walden community during the two years they had been around. After the murder, many rumors started circulating that in there had, in fact, been "bad blood" between the brothers.

It was thought that Bill Grace murdered his brother Jack to prevent him from revealing to Fannie Andrews, Bill's fiancée in Walden, that Bill was already married to two other women. Bill lured Jack to Walden by telling him an actress friend of his wanted to see him that night. In addition to wanting to hide his marriages from Fannie, Bill may have also murdered his brother for his money. Bill would rob his brother in order to go on a fancy honeymoon with his third bride, Fannie Andrews. Jack seems to have been doing much better financially than Bill.

A slight twist here is that Jack was also a bigamist, but his conscience may have been getting the better of him. Back in Fall River, Jack had married Belle Shadock, a well known piano player. Belle had left Jack, but they had never divorced. She claimed she hid from him because he was abusive. Jack had since taken Helen Burgess as his wife and they lived at 7 Washington Place in Newburgh, New York. It was Helen who testified that when Jack Grace left their apartment, headed for

The Grace Murder Case

Walden, he had $320 on him and was also wearing two diamond rings and a diamond cluster pin. These items and the money were not found on Jack Grace's body and would be instrumental in the trial.

This sketch is from the September 16, 1912 edition of *The Newburgh Daily News*. The caption underneath the picture says it was made at the Newburgh jail by Burton F. Gillette for *The Daily News*.

The Case

The day after Jack's body was discovered, the September 12, 1912 edition of *The Newburgh Daily News* said, "The murder, though happening in the business center of the village, was not discovered until 7:30 the evening of September 11, 1912. As a result of stench coming from the club room, Ralph Balldon, a member of the club, and "Sunny" Corcoran, employed in the cigar store down stairs, went up to investigate; thinking that perhaps a stray cat had died in the rooms somewhere." [iii]

The murder took place at the Twentieth Century Club rooms, which were in a building on the south side of Main Street, near the intersection with Ulster Avenue. Today, this building is a vacant office building. The club rooms were not used a great deal in the summer months, but were quite popular during the winter when games and music were enjoyed by the twenty young men who were members. They each paid dues in order to use the rooms and maintain them. The papers said that the lock on the entrance door which had been broken for two months prior to the murder had not been fixed and the electric lights in the chandelier that had burned out had not been replaced, so the two boys who discovered the body needed to light matches to look around.

"The Club consisted of a large front room facing Main Street with two smaller rooms in the rear. In the one to the left were a stove and wash bowl. The rear room to the right with entrances from either of the other rooms was used as a game room. Chairs surrounded the table in the center of this room and a couch was to the left of the door entering from the main room. It was towards this couch that the boys, groping through the dark rooms, were drawn by the strong stench."[iv]

The Newburgh Daily News continued with: "As Balldon got down on his knees to peer under the couch, he observed a man's hand. 'My God! Sunny it's a dead man!' gasped Balldon. Jumping up in his fright, Balldon thrust "Sunny" to one side so

The Grace Murder Case

hard that it knocked the latter down, his feet sliding under the couch, striking the corpse."[v]

The boys ran down the narrow steps to the street, where Officer Dill Ronk, the chief's brother and Thomas Terwilliger, owner of the cigar store, heard their screams and went up to investigate.

"Officer Ronk pulled the couch over exposing a medium height, heavily set man with black, curly hair, lying face down on the floor in a terrible condition. His body was badly decomposed and a pool of blood saturated the carpet under his head."[vi]

According to *The Newburgh Daily News*, "Jack's right arm was thrown over his head, concealing a gaping wound in the crown of his head. His left arm lay under the body and his left leg was crossed over his outstretched right leg. On top of his prostrate body laid a panama hat, free from blood or other marks. His pockets were inside out as if they had been searched."[vii]

As soon as Chief George Ronk saw the body, he identified it as that of Jack Grace. *The Newburgh Daily News* said that Jack made an enviable reputation as a wrestler by defeating such men as Joe Zellar, Young Sandow, Kid Parker, Young Prokus, a Greek wonder, and also Tom Jenkins in an exhibition bout that the Elks Minstrels held in the Didsbury Opera House. The Didsbury Theatre was only a few doors down from where Jack's body was found. Jack Grace's wrestling name was "Strangler Jack." It also said that "Grace was employed at the Terrace Inn, a Walden restaurant and bar, for several months as a bartender while living in Walden. He had since moved to Newburgh and was bartending there while training for a wrestling match."[viii]

The Case

This is the building where Jack Grace was murdered as it looks today. The Twentieth Century Club was on the second floor and Terwilligers Cigar store was on the first. The only remnant of the original building is the paneling next to the entrance door; the rest has been sided with vinyl. Photo by Lisa Melville.

The Grace Murder Case

The next morning, the crime scene was examined more carefully. It was found that Jack Grace was killed while he was sleeping in a Morris chair in the corner of the front room nearest to the Walker building. His murderer had apparently sat talking with him in the room lighted only by the light from Main Street and waited for Jack to fall asleep. Perhaps the killer even went to lie down on the couch under which he would later hide Jack's body.

At the trial, Chief Ronk testified that "the room smelled so bad we had to throw stuff around before we could stay in the room. Everything was scattered with blood, the carpet and windows. You could see blood scattered against one of the front windows next to Main Street, the walls and cushion were all soaked with blood and the cuspidor was half full of blood. The galvanized tin pail was all covered with blood; the covering over the couch where his body was found was soaked with blood."[ix]

Police speculated that after Jack fell asleep, the murderer went cautiously to the left, rear room and grabbed the meat cleaver which was used by the club members to cut kindling wood. The killer then crept upon Jack asleep in the chair and, with a strong blow, nearly split his head in two.

Since the chair cushions were soaked in blood, it was believed that when Jack Grace was struck from behind his body slid down to the floor. His head resting for a time on the seat of the Morris chair, soaking the cushion with blood and, as the body gave a last convulsive jerk, it fell against the sidewall, staining the wall paper with blood.

Jack was then robbed of $320, two diamond rings, and a diamond pin. His body was dragged to the other room where he was placed on the floor. The couch was put on top of him and pressed down to its original position, causing Jack's features to become distorted as if he had been flattened. During the

The Case

investigation, Chief Ronk found two diamond rings and a diamond pin hidden under the soap in Bill Grace's shaving mug that was in the suitcase he used for his honeymoon. Bill said that his brother Jack had given him the rings and pin for safekeeping and that when he heard of the murder he hid them fearing that it would look bad for him to have them.

After robbing Jack, the murderer then retrieved the pail from the adjoining rear room and tried to clean up the scene. The meat cleaver was wiped off, but there were remnants of hair, flesh, and blood stains still attached to it.

Eugene Lupton (also spelled as John Litlon in the court transcript - there are many spelling errors and summaries instead of verbatim transcription in the transcript), Mike Deegan, Frank Hargian and Fred Fox were all in front of the Walden Savings Bank around 6:10 A.M. on September 8, 1912. The bank was on the corner diagonally across from the Twentieth Century Club building and they could see the front of it clearly from where they stood. They had heard noises coming from the Twentieth Century Club rooms and had seen what looked like a hand wiping something away on the window of the club rooms. Fred Fox, being a member of the club, went up to investigate, but found the door was locked and his key did not work. Had the murderer really come this close to being caught in the act?

The chief of police, George M. Ronk, was considered the founder of the Walden Police Department and he was the main detective in this case. Chief Ronk raised the local police department from a one man force to a body of several men, introduced uniforms to the officers, and eventually became Chief. His brother, Dill Ronk, was one of his officers.

The "Chief" was a large man, standing more than six feet tall. Although he never attended the State Police Academy, locals of the time said he seemed to possess a sixth sense when it came to solving a crime. Ronk was a legend in the village, but he failed to deliver any hard evidence in this case and it was such a messy scene, there must have been physical evidence. Of course, DNA testing was not available, but finger printing had been around for years. By 1903, New York State prisons began the first systematic use of fingerprinting, but there was nothing in the court transcripts about fingerprint evidence, even though there was a newspaper article that mentioned fingerprints.

The September 17, 1912 edition of the *Fall River Daily Globe* stated that "Finger prints left by the slayer of "Jack" Grace in the Athletic club were discovered today by detectives here. The wood and linen on which they were found will be sent to an expert, together with marks of the fingers of Antone (known as "Bill") Grace, now in jail at Newburg[h], charged with the murder of his brother."[x] This evidence was never presented at the trial - why? Was it because the prints did not match Bill Grace's fingerprints? Or did something else prevent this evidence from being used?

The transcript includes testimony from Talcott C. Vanamee, a city of Newburgh physician who had experience in testing blood. He had examined the diamond ring found in Bill Grace's shaving kit. He found a little red spot about the size of the head of a pin. This was red and had all the external earmarks of a clot of blood. He examined it under a microscope and testified it was blood. He also performed a chemical test that proved it was blood, but they did not have the knowledge or technology then that could identify whether it was human blood or that of some other mammal.

Chief Ronk testified about the contents of the "honeymoon" suitcase Fannie Andrews had shown him. Bill Grace had borrowed the suitcase from Fannie's brother-in-law, Edgar VanKeuran. Bill left the suitcase with Fannie when he returned to Walden after being notified of his brother's death.

The Case

Chief George Ronk of the Walden Police Department and the chief detective on the Grace Murder Case. Photo courtesy of Marcus Millspaugh.

The Grace Murder Case

Chief Ronk said that he examined the suitcase's contents in the presence of Officer Dill Ronk, the chief's brother and Charles Young, a reporter. He found a man's suit of dark clothes, some men's shirts, and a shaving cup. At the trial, he identified the shaving cup as the one he had found in the suitcase. In the soap cake of the shaving cup, he found two diamond rings and a pin, which were also presented as evidence. The pin and rings were entirely under the soap in a piece of paper. Several witnesses testified that this jewelry was similar to what they saw on Jack Grace, but no one actually said they were one hundred percent sure that it was Jack's jewelry. However, Louis Kades, a jeweler in Newburgh testified that it was the ring that he had reset for Jack Grace in June of 1912.

Several witnesses testified that Bill Grace always tried to borrow money and he was behind on several bills, but Fannie Andrews testified that her husband had left her in New York City with three $50 bills when he returned to Walden. That Monday and Tuesday (this would have been September 9th and 10th) before their marriage, they had gone to the city and Bill Grace had paid for all the expenses. The last time Jack Grace was seen alive was on Saturday, September 7th. She said he did not purchase anything for himself on that trip, but he did buy her a willow plume for her hat for which he paid $10. After coming back from this two day trip, they were married on the 11th and went back to the city to honeymoon. The only sketch of Fannie at the trial shows her in a hat with a feather plume. Was she wearing the feather that Bill had bought for her?

Fannie went on to state that they had gone to the theatre the night of their wedding trip and they did not return to the hotel until eleven or twelve o'clock, which is when they heard of Jack's death. The next morning, Bill Grace took her to her cousin's house in the city and left alone to return to Walden.

The Case

Bill Grace in his court testimony says that when he first came to Walden, he boarded at Terwilliger's Boarding house on Orchard Street. Perhaps this is how Fannie and Bill met since Fannie's mother, a knife industry worker's widow, also had a boarding house on Orchard Street. He soon moved to Fanny Kidd's Boarding House on James Street and was still there in September of 1912. Fanny testified at Grace's trial, attended most of the trial, and *The Newburgh Daily News* claimed that Bill Grace wrote to her at least once a week from prison. She said she liked Bill because he was kind to her elderly husband.

Jonathan D. Wilson, the prosecutor for the State, tried to show that Bill suddenly had money and was spending it and also tried to piece together what he was doing during these days in September. "Leaving his fiancée at her home, Grace called at Palenthorpe & Wilkinson's clothing store, where after examining his wedding suit and finding it satisfactory, he purchased a dress shirt and paid a bill of $30, with three $10 bills, at the same time holding out a $50 bill that he desired Palenthorpe to change for him."[xi] William Palenthorpe was a tailor with a shop on Main Street.

"On Wednesday afternoon a short time before the hour of his marriage Bill Grace was talking to a local person on Lustig's corner, directly opposite the scene of the alleged crime. While talking, he kept drawing a semi-circle on the walk with the toe of his shoe and casting nervous glances up at the club room. At that time no attention was paid to these peculiar actions but the later developments caused the local person to recall them."[xii] This was obviously not admissible in court, but the papers were filled with this kind of rhetoric.

When Bill Grace returned to his boarding house, Mrs. Kidd had her back toward the door and was busy working in the kitchen and, for that reason, did not notice whether Bill was carrying anything when he came in the house.

The Grace Murder Case

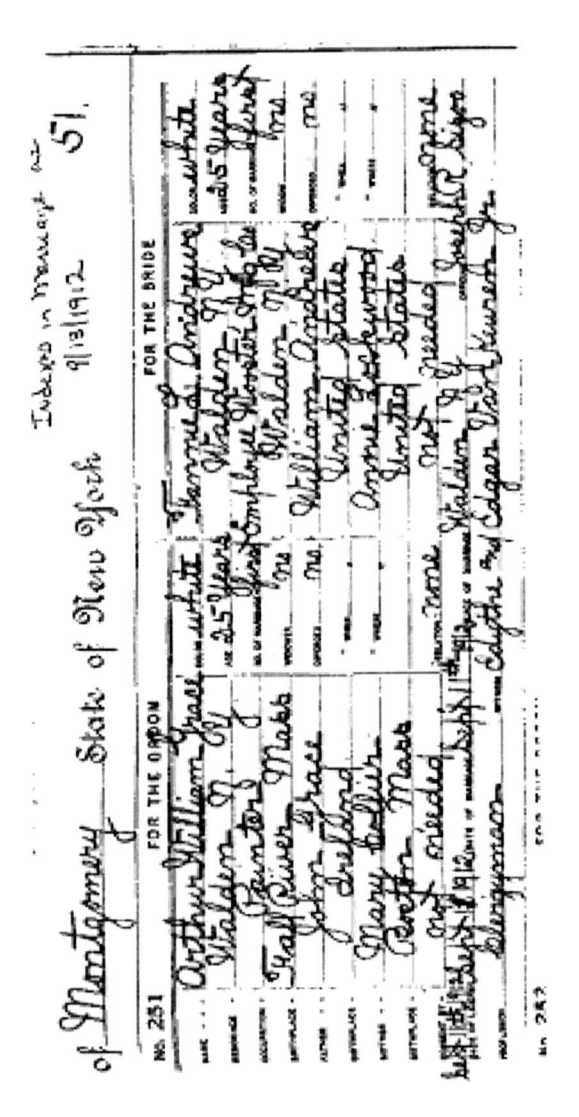

Marriage Record of Fannie Andrews and Bill Grace from the Town of Montgomery Town Hall.

The Case

Grace remained in the house until a little after eleven o'clock that morning, when he went out. He returned at about 7:30 P.M. and was in and out of the house several times, but did not sleep there that night. He next appeared there on Tuesday night to pack the suitcase he borrowed from Edgar VanKeuren, his future brother-in-law. As he was preparing to depart, Mrs. Kidd asked him if the rumor of his marriage were true and he replied that he was getting married on Wednesday.

About eight o'clock the next morning, the day of his wedding, Grace asked Mrs. Kidd if he might burn some garbage in the backyard. She consented and Grace then spent some time burning articles in the backyard. It was believed that he burned his blood stained clothes at that time, but no evidence was found in the ashes.

After he was done, Grace returned to the house and asked Mrs. Kidd to have water heated for a bath by eleven o'clock. At 9:30, Bill Grace went down the street, taking another suitcase and an overcoat, which he left at Fannie Andrew's house. At 11:10 A.M. he returned to the Kidd Boarding house for his bath and at 2:00 P.M., he and Fannie were married at the Dutch Reformed Church. They left for their honeymoon shortly after a small reception at the Andrews residence that Fannie's mother hosted for them on Orchard Street.

When the police searched Grace's room at the boarding house at 11 James Street, they found photographs of girls and a number of obscene post cards. Bill Grace had not been to this boarding house to sleep from August 27th until Tuesday, September 10th, the night after his return with his fiancée from a shopping trip to New York.

Eye witness accounts were relied on at the trial according to the transcripts and it is curious that there were so many people roaming the village streets so early in the morning, between 3:00 A.M. and 5:00 A.M. on September 8, 1912. Most people would be sleeping. One does not think of that when you think of 1912, but maybe it was not as quiet as we think in the "good, old days."

In 1912, Walden was a thriving village. This was before World War I, before prohibition, and before the depression. William Howard Taft was president and the country was experiencing the birth of social reform. It really was quite an amazing year: the Titanic sank and women suffragists were lobbying hard for the vote. Thomas Edison was still alive and electrical lighting in homes was still a fairly new thing. Henry Ford introduced the Model T in 1906, but the assembly line was not introduced until 1913, so there would have been some cars on the streets of Walden, but the streetcars or trolleys and horse drawn wagons were the prominent mode of transportation. The trolley went straight through Walden and the tracks were right in the middle of Main Street.

The trolleys operated from 6:00 A.M. to 11:00 P.M. daily, and a trip to Walden would take an average of forty minutes from Orange Lake in Newburgh. Eight round-trips from Newburgh to Walden were made each day. The 11:00 P.M. trolley was from Newburgh to Walden, and the conductor and the motorman would stay overnight in Walden. The 6:00 A.M. trolley left Walden for Newburgh and was one of the primary means of transportation for employees who worked in Newburgh.

Walden has always been a "blue-collar" community. The Wallkill River runs right through the center of the village and provided a superior source of power, so it was a natural place for early industrial development that needed hydropower. It was also inevitable that a village would develop around this source to house a workforce. After the gristmills, the woolen industry took advantage of the Wallkill's power. Jacob T. Walden started a very successful woolen mill in an old gristmill in 1813 and the village was renamed Walden in his honor. Originally, it had been called Wilemantown and, later, Kiddtown after other early settlers of the area. Henry Wileman, whose name had first graced the village, Wilemantown, was forgotten when Walden became Kiddtown. These early settlements, although successful, were not very large, but both Wileman and Kidd were very common family names in the area and can still be found today.

The postcard above shows west Main Street and the trolley. Postcard courtesy of Marcus Millspaugh.

By 1856, the woolen industry had declined, making way for the knife works. The first knife factory to come to Walden in 1856 was the New York Knife Factory. After that, two other large factories, the Walden Knife Company and Schrade, were formed to produce knives, giving the village the nickname of the "Little Sheffield" after Sheffield in England, which was known for its fine cutlery. In fact, there were many immigrants

The Grace Murder Case

from England in Walden who hoped to take advantage of the trade and plentiful work. This was a specialized skill and it was passed down in families. Many of the people who testified in the Grace case were in the knife business.

By 1913, 804 people, or 19 percent of the entire village, worked in the knife factories. In 1913, 327 individuals worked in the New York Knife Company, 340 in the Walden Knife Company and 137 employees in the Schrade Knife Company.[xiii]

There were also other factories in the village. In 1876, the Wooster Manufacturing Company was organized by Hiram Wooster and George Stoddard and became the first company to make pants for working men. String Cooper claims in his *History of Walden* booklet that they were the second company to make overalls in New York State.

For many years, Wooster's was one of Walden's most successful manufacturing industries. It later became a hat factory, an underwear factory, the Eastern plant for the Royal Furniture Company, and the home of the Active Specialty Company. In 1912, it was still an overall factory and Fannie Andrews worked there before her marriage to Bill Grace.

There were few child labor laws, so these factories would have included many child workers. Men in 1912 worked on the average 63 hours per week, the women worked between 58 and 63 hours per week, and the children worked 51 hours or less per week.[xiv]

The knife industry was one of the best paid. Although there were different pay rates for adult men, adult women, and children, the wage scales for each category were above the wages paid in other industries. The average wage scale from 1860 to 1875 for adult males was $36 a month, for adult females $18 per month, males under age 18 were $15, and females under age 18 were $12 a month. By 1880, the wages were $60.75 a month for skilled labor and $40.50 per month for ordinary workers. The work week during this period consisted of six ten-hour days and, unlike many factories during this period, the New York Knife Company operated year round.

To put these wages in perspective, the average wage for manufacturing skilled workers in 1900 was $435 a year or $33.50 a month, and for unskilled labor was only $22 a month, so Walden Knife workers were being paid well above the average manufacturing salary as early as 1860.[xv]

This was a manufacturing town and it was hopping. This was the place that Jack and Bill Grace decided to settle down, at least for a while. Fall River, Massachusetts, their home town, was also very industrial at this time. It was bigger than Walden and maybe the Grace boys thought they could make their fortune in Walden and Newburgh; but maybe they were both running from their past.

New York Knife Factory. Postcard courtesy of Marcus Millspaugh.

The Grace Murder Case

Walden Knife Factory. Photo courtesy of Marcus Millspaugh.

Schrade Knife Company. Postcard courtesy of Marcus Millspaugh.

28

The Case

After working such long hours, it was little wonder that the village had a thriving social business; there were plenty of places to get a drink and play cards and talk. There were two large hotels, the Eagle and the Saint Nicholas. Jesse Wade, the bartender at the Eagle, testified that Jack and Bill had come in for a drink the night Jack was murdered and that he had mentioned he was hoping to meet up with an actress.

There was a housing shortage and many boarding houses opened for the workers of the factories and it was common at the time to open up a few rooms in your house to make extra money. For many widows, like Fannie Andrews' mother, boarding was the only source of income. It was acceptable for young girls to work in factories, but once they married, they stopped working if they could. Many women, especially those with large families, found it necessary to work outside the home, but those with houses often ran them as a boarding house to support themselves and their families. Older children would also contribute to the household by working at the factories.

Many social clubs existed in Walden, such as the Twentieth Century Club. These groups rented rooms and had meetings. The Twentieth Century Club was a place for "the boys" to go and play cards whenever they wanted; you paid dues and got a key to the room. Terwilliger's Cigar Store was on the first floor of the building and a handy place to grab a smoke, especially before a card game.

The court transcripts do not indicate that any other suspects investigated, even though Bill Grace said that the last time he saw his brother he was with a man named "Connelly". He said that Connelly did not have the best reputation. It is mentioned in Bill Grace's testimony, but there is no mention of police investigating it. The December 13, 1912 edition of *The Newburgh Daily News*, says "A weak spot in the defense was the failure to bring out more enlightenment on the subject of the man "Connelly" who, according to "Bill" Grace, was the last person seen with "Jack." There has been an impression that he was a mythical personage, but plenty of evidence can be secured to show that he was a real man, "The Fighting Blacksmith", and had appeared in a pugilistic encounter in Newburgh, and was known to be a friend of "Jack" Grace."[xvi]

The papers continued to report daily on the case and some odd things were mentioned that never made it to trial. Such as the September 16, 1912 article of the *Newburgh Daily News*, which said: "It was learned last night that about midnight, on the eve of the murder, Officer Dill Ronk in making his rounds in the rear of the Terwilliger building, the scene of the murder, discovered a pair of long skids used by the Walker grocery establishment next door in unloading heavy barrels and boxes in the rear of its store, placed up against the low roof of the Terwilliger building. Officer Ronk informed Terwilliger of this fact and the latter went into his back yard and returned the skids to where they belonged. It is believed that the murderer had placed the skids where they were found with the intention later abandoned, of getting "Jack" Grace's body down to the alley in the rear of the building, and thus out to Orchard Street, where he would make it appear a case of highway robbery or an automobile accident."[xvii]

Another article from the September 21, 1912 *Middletown Daily Argus* tries to link the murder to the mafia in an article titled "Chief Ronk Warned by Black Hand."[xviii] It seems that the Chief received a postcard in the mail claiming that Anthony Grace was innocent and warned the chief not to be anxious to convict the prisoner under penalty of dire punishment. No signature was attached to the card which was postmarked from the city of Poughkeepsie. The Chief did not take the threat seriously and it is not mentioned in any other paper.

The Case

The St. Nicholas Hotel on Main Street in Walden. The building were the Grace Murder took place is to the right of the brick building across the street. The St. Nicholas is gone; this is now the present site of the Walden Federal Bank. Postcard courtesy of Marcus Millspaugh.

This article continues to say that the Twentieth Century Club rooms opened for the season on September 15th, this would have been only days after the discovery of the body. It says "The old Tambar phonograph which has been silent for some time was again in evidence and the fact that a murder had occurred there within a few days seemed to be forgotten by the members."[xix] Today, this would have been unheard of; the crime scene would still be controlled and under investigation. Also, the description of the room was so bloody that it is hard to believe the rooms would have been cleaned up in such a short period of time.

The October 1, 1912 edition of *The Newburgh Daily News* wrote, "Dorothy Brokaw, a slim, brown-haired little chorus girl, appeared in the Didsbury Theatre on Saturday night, May 6,

1911, with the 'Campaigners' a musical comedy." Dorothy Brokaw, with other members of the troupe roomed in the house of Mr. and Mrs. Alonzo Van Scoyk, on Main Street overnight.

Jack Grace was also a roomer in the house of the Van Scoyk's at the time the 'Campaigners' showed here. Dorothy Brokaw, observing Jack Grace going down the stairs, asked Mrs. Van Scoyk who 'that fellow' was and was told he was Jack Grace, a wrestler who was giving wrestling exhibitions in the Didsbury Opera House from time to time. It then developed that Dorothy was not only acquainted with Jack Grace, but she also knew Jack Grace's musical wife, Belle Shadrack, from whom Jack was separated in Providence, Rhode Island, and with whom it is alleged 'Bill' Grace was caught having an affair by Jack Grace, the incident resulting in bad blood existing between the two brothers as was stated by the police of Fall River as well as the Grace family."[xx] The article also indicated that this may have been the girl that Jack Grace had come to Walden to see the night of his murder. She was not a witness at the trial and no mention was made of a police interview with her, which is surprising because if she was with Jack the night of his death, that would be significant.

Both local and major metropolitan newspapers in New York followed the Grace Murder case and oftentimes the information and story details conflicted with one another, although the main story is quite consistent. It seemed this was a form of entertainment since people have a fascination with gore and intrigue; the papers took advantage of such a sensational story to sell papers. This phenomenon in human behavior has changed little and is still very much true today.

The Grace Murder case was all that was talked about for a long time and then it was forgotten. Fanny Andrews never was asked for an interview or at least never granted one that was recorded, but we can still piece together much of the story.

The Case

The Eagle Hotel. Jack and Bill Grace stopped in for a drink here on September 7, 1912. Postcard courtesy of Marcus Millspaugh.

The Eagle Hotel in 2010. Photo by Lisa Melville.

The Grace Murder Case

However, the people are all gone, so firsthand knowledge by those involved is lost. We can only imagine and try to interpret how they felt. For instance, it must have been hard for Fannie to live the rest of her life in the same house on Orchard Street. It must have been embarrassing for a young girl to have been a victim of this man, even though it was obvious she was innocent.

The few relatives I was able to contact that remembered Fannie, knew something had happened, but it was understood that no one was to talk about it. Having it understood that a topic is not to be discussed implies distress or shame about it and over time this must have taken a toll. Fannie's story is looked at a little later as are the details of the case.

The Case

Miss Dorothy Brokaw, Actress
Picture of Dorothy Brokaw from the October 1, 1912 edition of the *Newburgh Daily News*.

[i] *Fall River Daily Globe*, September 16, 1912, p.1
[ii] *Newburgh Daily News*, December 10, 1912, p.1
[iii] *Newburgh Daily News*, September 12, 1912, p.1
[iv] *Newburgh Daily News*, September 12, 1912, p.1
[v] *Newburgh Daily News*, September 12, 1912, p.1
[vi] *Newburgh Daily News*, September 12, 1912, p.1
[vii] *Newburgh Daily News*, September 12, 1912, p.1
[viii] *Newburgh Daily News,* September 12, 1912, p.1
[ix] Court Transcript, p.50
[x] *Fall River Daily Globe,* September 17, 1912, p.1
[xi] *Newburgh Daily News*, September 14, 1912, p.1
[xii] *Newburgh Daily News*, September 14, 1912, p.1
[xiii] Sopko, Joseph. *New York Knife Company Cultural Resources Site Examination of New York State Museum*, 2002
[xiv] Sopko, Joseph. *New York Knife Company Cultural Resources Site Examination of New York State Museum,* 2002
[xv] Sopko, Joseph, *New York Knife Company Cultural Resources Site Examination of New York State Museum,* 2002
[xvi] *Newburgh Daily News*, December 13, 1912, p.1
[xvii] *Newburgh Daily News*, September 16, 1912, p.1
[xviii] *Middletown Daily Argus*, September 21, 1912, p.1
[xix] *Middletown Daily Argus*, September 21, 1912, p.1
[xx] *Newburgh Daily News,* October 1, 1912, p.1
[xx] Court Transcript, p.26

2

THE GRACE BROTHERS

John "Jack" Grace's decomposing body was found on September 11, 1912 under a couch in the building that housed the Twentieth Century Club, a club he belonged to made up of young men who liked to gamble, play cards, drink, and hang out together. He had massive head wounds, but the rest of his body was untouched. The *Orange County Times Press* reported on September 12th that: "In the pockets of the dead man's clothing were found a New York Central time table, advertising matter, pencils, handkerchiefs, a girl's photograph, cigars, a memorandum book, two knives, a bunch of keys, a return ticket to Newburgh, theatre checks, a button photo of himself and ten cents in change."[1] The return ticket means Jack intended to return to his Newburgh home and to his wife, Helen Grace.

Jack Grace and Bill Grace were brothers and, by most accounts, were quite friendly. They grew up in Fall River, Massachusetts. Their Portuguese parents, John and Mary Grace, had settled in Fall River and were raising a family of five kids. Both brothers had come to Walden sometime in 1910. Jack had tried various jobs in Walden, one article saying that he had tried to open a restaurant, but he settled in Newburgh as a bartender at the Metropolitan Hotel.

Jack Grace had made a name for himself as a wrestler, or pugilist, and was known as "Strangler" Jack. He had been a champion wrestler, in his weight, of the New England States and had traveled extensively for this popular sport. Amongst his belongings were many awards and newspapers clippings of his

The Grace Murder Case

fights. He had continued to wrestle while in Walden and Newburgh in Orange County, New York.

The murder victim, Jack Grace from the August 4, 1913 edition of the Newburgh Daily News.

Bill Grace admits being with his brother before his death. He was also seen the Sunday morning after the night Jack was believed to have been killed, leaving the building where his brother's body was found by an employee of the cigar store which was in the same building on the first floor. Bill was accused of his brother's murder, was tried and found guilty, being executed by electric chair for the crime. What happened between them in those early morning hours of Sunday,

The Grace Brothers

September 8, 1912 will never be fully known. We can only imagine that there was some kind of altercation between them. Someone killed John "Jack" Grace - the most likely suspect was his brother, but Bill Grace did point to another possibility.

Bill Grace insisted that he was innocent and he was convicted on purely circumstantial evidence. He implicated a possible suspect known as Jimmy O'Connell, better known as "Kid," a pugilist of considerable fame in Orange County. It had been rumored that the two wrestlers, Jack Grace and Jimmy O'Connell, had been fighting. Both Jack and Jimmy were employed at the Metropolitan Hotel in Newburgh.

Today, they would have applied modern forensics to the case. The description of the crime scene was so bloody, there would have been an incredible amount of physical evidence to either prove or disprove Bill Grace's guilt. But in 1912, that technology was not available. There were many observations in the different papers, but many did not make it to the trial. For example, the *Orange County Times*, September 12, 1912 edition says, "The condition of the room indicated that a card game had been in progress as cards, poker chips and chairs were strewn about the floor. Lying under Grace's face was his watch. Further investigation revealed that he had a receipt of the Order of Eagles which shows that on August 31st he paid $2.50 to Secretary Edward D. Reagan, of Fall River Aerie, No. 570."[ii]

Both Jack and Bill Grace seemed to move around a lot for work, but perhaps it was more likely that they were trying to evade their wives. Jack worked mostly as a bartender and he seemed to be doing quite well. While still in Walden, before moving to Newburgh, he worked at the Terrace Inn and there was reference to him starting a restaurant. Bell Chadwick, his first and only legal wife, said he had lost a business that his mother set him up in Pawtucket, Rhode Island. While Jack seemed to be very personable, athletic, and outgoing, all good skills to be a successful bartender, he seemed to lack the skills necessary to run his own business.

Jack Grace had several wrestling matches in the Didsbury Theater while he was in Walden and Newburgh. The Didsbury was located just a few doors down from where Jack Grace was murdered. Postcard courtesy of Marcus Millspaugh.

Jack Grace was no angel - he was also a bigamist. He was married to Miss Belle Chadwick in 1905, but had married Helen Burgess in March of 1912 and they lived together at 7 Washington Place in Newburgh.

The Grace Brothers

In an interview done by a correspondent from Fall River with Jack's first wife, you get some insight into his personality or character. Of course, you have to consider that this is from a former wife and take that into consideration. The September 17, 1912 edition of *The Fall River Daily Globe* says:

> A reporter called at the home of Mr. and Mrs. Louis Chadwick at 340 County Street this morning in an effort to substantiate the report that "Jack" Grace already had a wife living in this city and that she was a daughter of the above couple. A young woman answered the door and replied that she was Mrs. "Jack" Grace. In a conversation later, Mrs. Grace stated that she had known "Jack" Grace for many years before she became married to him, giving the date as Nov. 5 1905, of the marriage, and which is substantiated by the records of the city clerk. The ceremony was performed by the Rev. Mathias S. Kauffman at his home at 131 Rock Street, the clergyman being pastor of St. Paul's M.E. church at the time.
>
> If Jack Grace has married another woman in Newburgh since he left this city, he is a bigamist," said Mrs. Grace, "As I have never been legally separated from him. A number of times I sought to secure a divorce, but was unable to do so because he refused to sign certain papers.
>
> In further explanation, Mrs. Grace said that shortly after her marriage to Grace, they left this city and went to New York City. While there Grace was of a shiftless nature, and refused to do anything in the line of work, while she was forced to work for 11 hours at a stretch playing the piano in a theatre, after which he took her money from her. His treatment of her at that time was

The Grace Murder Case

nothing short of brutal, she states and adds that neighbors in the vicinity of where they were living in Jersey City threatened to interfere when he started to abuse her.

When the news of the murder first reached the local Mrs. Grace through the newspaper accounts, she noted the fact that a woman who represented herself as the wife of the dead wrestler and who lived in Newburgh, was to look after the interests of the murdered man. To this the local wife states that she is the only lawful wife of the murdered man, and she has written to the Newburgh authorities stating that fact and which has also served to bring to light the fact that 'Jack' Grace was also a bigamist at the time he threatened to expose his brother Anthony when the latter was about to marry for the third time. [iii]

From another article in the *Fall River Daily Globe* on September 18, 1912, Belle continues that:

Jack was always his mother's favorite son. His mother owns considerable property in Fall River and she set him up in business in Pawtucket when he was little over 18 years old. He ran a saloon at the corner of Gardner and Main streets in Pawtucket. His mother swore that he was over 21 years of age and he was granted a license. To my certain knowledge Jack was voting in Fall River when he was but 18 years old. He lost his business in Pawtucket and later we went to New York [sic].

It is five years now since I have seen him. I have heard of him from time to time. He has asked my mother, repeatedly, to tell him where I was. But mother knew what I suffered at his hands. It may not seem right to talk this way about him now that he is dead, but I cannot forget the suffering I endured. I have always worked. I have been willing and anxious to work but at least a part of the money belonged to me. I worked for hours playing the piano in moving picture houses, sometimes so tired that I was ready to drop. I have also posed for artists and I worked in Siegel's. I was able to make my way alone and I was much happier so. Life with him became one long nightmare."[iv]

However, people are complicated, having both good and bad qualities. From the second Mrs. Jack Grace, we learn that Jack seemed to be concerned about his brother ruining another young woman's life. She stated at the trial that, "I recall the defendant, William Grace, coming to my house during September and John Grace had a conversation with him in my presence, the conversation was mostly relating to the trip they were planning to Fall River over Labor day weekend. One conversation was about marrying. He was asked if he meant to marry Fannie Andrews or not."[v]

Helen said that Bill assured Jack he was not going to marry Fannie. "He said he was going there for friendship. Jack said if he did intend to marry her he would appear and tell he had another wife. William said he did not intend to marry the girl. That was all that was said about the marriage."[vi]

In her testimony, she confirmed that as far as she knew, John and William were friendly and that William had gone to their house on several occasions. So if there was any truth to the story that Bill had an affair with Jack's first wife, it would seem that they had patched things up with each other.

Helen Grace also testified at the trial that when he left their home on September 7, 1912 around 7:00 P.M., he carried with

The Grace Murder Case

him $320 and was wearing two diamond rings and a diamond cluster pin. This is a lot to spend in one evening in the 21st century, so in 1912, it was extreme.

Helen continued her testimony and said at the trial that she was quite pleased that the court had convicted the right man. She did not seem fond of her brother-in-law, William. She told the court that she and Jack Grace were married on March 9, 1912 somewhere in the vicinity of City Hall in Jersey City. She said she didn't know who had married them, that she supposed him to be a minister. She did not have a certificate of marriage; she said she had left all the details to her husband. So we really do not know if there was an actual certificate of marriage issued.

The rest of Jack's family seemed to have cared for him. His brother and brother-in-law came to Walden as soon as they heard of his death and made arrangements to bring his body home to Fall River. The body of Jack Grace was buried from D. & M. J. Coughlin's undertaking rooms. The burial was at Oak Grove cemetery, and was conducted under the auspices of a delegation from the local aerie of Eagles. Grace was a member of the local aerie and it was through the death benefit paid by the order to his widow that it was made possible to bring the body back to Fall River for interment.

The Grace Brothers

Mrs. Marie Burgess Grace

Sketch of Helen or Marie Grace from the trial from the Newburgh Daily News.

As for Antone William Grace, most of the materials written about the case portray him as being guilty well before his trial. The newspapers make him into an unfeeling monster, while only a few show a more human figure. As I researched the case, I started thinking it was possible that he was innocent, but Mr. Grace was probably a sociopath, and, in fact, had charmed me from the grave as he had done with so many during his short life. Bill Grace was deceptive, charming, manipulative, self-centered, and generally unable to bond deeply with others, lacking empathy or remorse and went through serial relationships.

Antone's parents, John and Mary A. Grace, lived at 548 Palmer Street in Fall River, Massachusetts. His childhood seems to be quite ordinary, at least on the surface. He was baptized in St. Patrick's church on January 25, 1887 by the Reverend T.P. Grace. According to the record, he was baptized under the name of "Antone Grace." In the Grace family, there were four boys- John or "Jack", Joseph, Frank, and Antone, and one girl named Mary. Antone is Bill or William, and was referred to as Bill, Will, Arthur, Antone, Anthony, or Tony, all names he went by at various times and under various circumstances.

The Grace family seems to have been a typical, working class family. They were Portuguese and had settled in Fall River where there was a large Portuguese population that still resides there today. Both Jack and Tony worked and helped out with the household as soon as they could, for their mother was a widow by their teenage years. Fall River was an industrial town and both brothers worked for a while at the Fall River Bleachery, one of the biggest employers in town.

The Grace Brothers

St. Patrick's Church and Rectory, Fall River, Massachusetts, where Antone Grace was baptized. Postcard courtesy of Lisa Melville.

Both Jack and Bill Grace worked in Walden when they first arrived in New York, but Jack had moved to Newburgh and was working as a bartender at the time of his death. Bill Grace was employed as a painter and had been working for the same contractor his entire time in Walden.

It was on January 6, 1908, at the age of 21, that Antone Grace was married to Annie Jones in Fall River. They had three children. She would be dead by his 25th birthday. He was married on October 9, 1910 in Lowell, Massachusetts for a second time to Jennie Shrigley under the alias of Arthur Brooks and deserted her before the birth of a child. Obviously, there was a bit of overlap and hastiness in these relationships. He was in Walden by 1911 and married Fannie Andrews on September 11, 1912 under the name of Arthur William Grace. He never divorced his first wife, so the second and third marriages were not legal. The bigamist changed his name each time he got

The Grace Murder Case

married. Perhaps he thought in some confused, misguided way that this made it ok, but he was probably just trying to make it more difficult to get caught. In fact, if Jack had not been murdered, he would probably not have gotten caught for bigamy. There is no way of knowing how long Bill Grace would have stayed in Walden with Fannie or how many other women he would have fooled into marriage after he abandoned her.

Once Bill Grace was apprehended for the murder of his brother, his life changed forever and the newspapers speculated about every aspect of this crime and his short life. Until that point, it seems that both the Grace boys were hardworking and generally liked in Walden. At the trial, Officer Dill Ronk said of Bill Grace: "I did not know anything against his reputation. I heard people talk about him since and what was said wasn't proper or good."[vii] The case revealed much about both Jack and Bill Grace's personal lives. Not only did it tell of Bill Grace and his multiple marriages, it revealed that Jack Grace was also a bigamist. There was some speculation that there was bad blood between Jack and Antone. There was a rumor that Jack's first wife, Belle Chadwick, and Antone had an affair. Belle Chadwick vehemently denied this in the September 18, 1912 edition of the *Fall River Daily Globe* article, saying, "It was bad enough to have to put up with Jack let alone be linked to his brother Anthony."[viii]

After hearing about Jack's death, Bill Grace returned alone from his honeymoon with Fannie Andrews and was arrested in Walden on Thursday, September 12, 1912 for the murder of his brother. He was brought to the Newburgh jail and returned to Walden for the last time for his inquest.

On September 27, 1912, Bill Grace was brought from the Newburgh jail manacled to Under Sheriff Lozier to an inquest at Supervisor R.G. Hume's office in Walden. He was being held

The Grace Brothers

without bail. This was huge news in the village of Walden as can be seen from this September 28th 1912 edition of the *Newburgh Daily News*:

> As soon as school was out - at 11:30 o'clock - children and some who were older began to assemble on the Second street side of Court House Square, the impression being that the prisoner was to be taken out that way in an automobile. Along toward 12 o'clock, however, the crowd shifted its location to the front, or Grand Street side of the Court House, the word having been passed around that the automobile was likely to start from there. A few minutes before 12 former Assemblyman De Forest Lozier, of Newark, N.J. accompanied by his wife and Mrs. Lozier's sister, came downstairs. They had been in Surrogate Swezey's court and were interested in the Richard Cunningham will contest. Mr. Lozier is a cousin of Under Sheriff Lozier. The trio wanted a glimpse of Grace and took seats in Deputy Sheriff Week's office.
>
> Grace wore a dark blue sack suit of clothes, with cuffs on his trousers, and a white shirt and collar and a black bow tie. His shoes were black and were newly shined. He had half of a big cigar in his mouth, which he was nervously puffing on.
>
> When Under Sheriff Lozier appeared Grace asked him for a dollar. Mr. Lozier went to the safe and got a $1 bill out of Grace's pile and a moment later handed it to him and Grace shoved it in his pocket, without even looking at it. Grace laughed and joked with Mr. Weeks as he did later when Mr. Lozier was adjusting the handcuffs. If remorse is eating the vitals of Anthony Grace there were no indications of it to the assembled

The Grace Murder Case

newspapermen present at this critical time in the fortunes and fate of the man before them.[ix]

This is the Newburgh Court House where Anthony was tried and convicted of his brother's murder. The addition in the back is the jail where Bill Grace was incarcerated from September 1912 until December 11, 1912 when he traveled down the river to Sing Sing. The courthouse still stands today and is in good shape. Postcard courtesy of Marcus Millspaugh.

Sheriffs Lozier and Weeks brought him back by automobile to be arraigned before Judge Holbrow. He was charged with the murder of Jack Grace and was held without bail for the Grand Jury. He was formally charged or indicted on October 22, 1912 by the Grand Jury of Orange County, Goshen, New York for the crime of Murder in the first degree. He was arraigned on the 23rd of October and pleaded not guilty. He was taken to the Newburgh jail and was held there until his trial in December of 1912. His trial took place in the Newburgh Courthouse.

The Grace Brothers

[i] *Orange County Times Press*, September 12, 1912, p.1
[ii] *Orange County Times*, September 12, 1912, p.1
[iii] *Fall River Daily Globe,* September 17, 1912 p.1
[iv] *Fall River Daily Globe*, September 18, 1912, p.1
[v] Court Transcript, p.31, 32
[vi] Court Transcript, p.32
[viii] *Fall River Daily Globe*, September 18, 1912, p.1
[ix] *Newburgh Daily News*, September 28, 1912, p.1

3

THE TRIAL

The trial took only two days to complete and that included the jury selection. Jury selection started the morning of December 9, 1912, and by 1:15 P.M., jury selection was over and the trial had begun. The trial was over by December 10th - the guilty verdict being read at 4:40 P.M.

The list of the jurymen as drawn, accepted, and sworn in was as listed on the following page. An article from the *Orange County Times- Press*, December 13, 1912 edition, talked about only six of those accepted. It listed their occupations and where they were from. It said, "The jury which will try Grace was selected from every walk of life. There are farmers, a merchant, an auctioneer, a shoemaker a painter a carpenter and a jeweler." It only went into detail on jurors 2, 3, 4, 5, 11 and 12.

Wilton Bennett was Antone William Grace's court appointed attorney. The Assistant District Attorney who prosecuted the case was Jonathan D. Wilson, Jr. The Judge overseeing the case was the Honorable Arthur S. Tompkins. All of these men were quite famous in their own right. The Judge, Arthur S. Tompkins, served on the Supreme Court from 1909 through 1935 and was also a member of Congress. Wilton Bennett was a well-known criminal defense lawyer from Port Jervis, New York, and also had his hands in local politics. He was an ardent Republican, served as a member of the County Central Committee and as Chairman of the Town Committee, and wrote the by-laws of the local Republican club. Assistant District Attorney Jonathan D. Wilton, Jr., was Chair of the Orange

The Trial

County Republican Party and, in 1928, was an alternate to the Republican National Convention.

Most of the evidence from the case seems to have disappeared, which is not surprising. After such cases were over, it was not uncommon for those involved or with access to any physical evidence to take souvenirs. Also, there were no local requirements on keeping the evidence at the time. Some of the evidence, such as the money and jewelry, would have been returned to the family or Jack's legal spouse, but there are no records of how his property was distributed.

As time went by, the case slowly became a vague reference. "Oh, the Grace case. Oh yeah, that was a murder in the village." Then, people might say what they remembered they had heard of it. It was the basic elements of the case: a man killed his brother and married this girl and went to the city on his honeymoon. Gone were the details of the trial and subsequent execution.

The prosecution laid out what they believed happened between September 7th and 11th, 1912, when Jack's body was found. They said Bill Grace lured his brother to Walden on Saturday, September 7th to meet an actress friend of his named Dorothy. Bill and Jack Grace were seen together for the last time that Saturday night. Bill insisted that he saw his brother on Sunday evening, September 8th, with a guy named Connolly. His story was never pursued at the trial.

The prosecution's theory was that Bill and Jack were at the Twentieth Century Club and that Bill killed Jack sometime early Sunday morning, September 8th. He then tried to clean up the scene and went home. He was seen leaving the Twentieth Century Club at 6:45 a.m. on that Sunday morning.

On Monday, September 9th, he took Fannie Andrews to New York City to sightsee and visit relatives; they returned on Tuesday, and on Wednesday the 11th, they were married. After

The Grace Murder Case

a small reception at the Andrews' home, they again left for New York City for their honeymoon. They were to continue on to Washington, DC. On Wednesday night after they returned from the theater, Bill got the call about his brother's murder.

THE JURY

No.1 Howard Brooks.

No. 2 Frank Miller: milk Dealer from Pine Bush who had read newspaper articles but had not formed an opinion.

No. 3. Edwin Leach: a farmer, who lived in the town of Warwick, said he believed in the death penalty and had read but little about the case and had formed no opinion.

No.4 M. G. Cooper: from Warwick, he is employed as a fireman and night watchman.

No. 5. Emanuel F. Kallian: shoemaker from Chester, Kallian is a sharp-featured intelligent looking little man with bright eyes and a very positive way of speaking. He said that he had no objections to the death penalty and that he had formed no opinion.

No. 6 H. G. Bush.

No. 7. Dewight Dutcher.

No. 8. Joseph C. Chamberlain.

No. 9 Wilmot Rumsey.

No. 10. Alonzo Weyant.

No. 11. Smith R. Decker: of Minisink, an auctioneer.

No. 12. J. Howard Durland: farmer, from Chester.[i]

The Trial

Men Who Will Decide the Fate of Anthony ("Bill") Grace, Charged With the Crime of Cain

Sketched In Court To-Day By Gillett

This sketch of the jury from the Grace Trial appeared in the December 11, 1912 edition of the Newburgh Daily News. Gillette did all the sketches for the trial.

55

The Grace Murder Case

Wilton Bennet

MANY FRIENDS ATTEND WILTON BENNET'S FUNERAL

Services of Elks Lodge Held at the

Picture of Wilton Bennet from his Obituary in the January 11, 1917 edition of the Port Jervis Evening Gazette.

The next morning, he left Fannie with $150 and their suitcases at her relative's home and returned to Walden where he was soon arrested for the murder. Fannie returned to Walden alone to face the truth about her new husband.

The Trial

The trial started with James Corcoran's testimony about discovering Jack Grace's body. Officer Dill Ronk's testimony followed. Dill Ronk was the brother of the Chief of Police. He was the first officer on the scene and went up to the room where the victim was found with Tom Terwilliger, owner of the cigar store on the first floor of the building. The paper says Corcoran worked at the store, but in the transcript the only employee of the store named is Charles Burlison. Corcoran however was a member of the Twentieth Century Club. By today's standards, bringing Terwilliger into the rooms immediately contaminated the scene, but in 1912, Officer Ronk would not have been thinking of that. After they had both seen the body, Officer Ronk went to get the Chief.

Sherwood Smith was a photographer with a shop on Main Street in Walden. He had taken photographs of the building where the Twentieth Century Club was housed. His photos of the different rooms and his pictures were evidence in the trial (exhibits No. 1, 2, 3, 4).[ii] Orange County would have returned the evidence to the police department. No records were kept by the Walden Police Department from this time, so none of these photographs were found. Also, Smith only took four pictures for the trial. One was of the exterior of the building and the other three were of the interior rooms of the Twentieth Century Club. This would have been a very helpful tool today to figure out what had happened since blood stain splatter and patterns can now be used to help analyze a crime scene. The transcript does not discuss the interior room pictures. They seem to have been taken after the body was removed and there is no mention of anything other than that they are a representation of the rooms.

The coroner's report at the time would be nothing like the detailed forensic reports done today, since forensic science has changed so dramatically from 1912. No official coroners report seems to have survived the nearly one hundred years since the crime; however, the trial transcript does talk about the murder scene.

The coroner was Fred G. Buss. Although he examined the body, he did not testify at the trial. It was another physician, Dr. Fred A. Hadley, who had gone to the Twentieth Century Club rooms. The trial transcript says:

> I am physician, was called to room Twentieth Century Club night of September 11th, 1912, to make examination of body which I did. Went there about nine o'clock and I found the body of a man lying on his face in one of the two rear rooms of the Twentieth Century Club Rooms. Later I examined the body in company of Coroner Buss and several others. Doctor Palen was there part of the time. I found two oblique gashes through the skull in the back part of it. The skull was fractured. The gashes were wide enough so I could put my fingers through them. They were absolutely through the skull. The brain tissue was presumable disturbed. From the examination of the wounds I made on this occasion the cause of death was compound fracture of the skull caused by these wounds. I looked at other parts of the body and it seemed to be in normal condition. I concluded from my examination the body had been dead 3 or 4 days. I base that on the fact that there was considerable filling up in the parts, rigor mortis had disappeared. This would indicate that from 3 to 5 days had disappeared; the outer skin on the chest had slopped a little. There were maggots on the body. I can only speak in approximate terms you understand [sic].[iii]

The Trial

He went on to say that: "The wounds were probably produced by some instrument that has a cutting edge, some instrument sharp enough to cut with, fairly heavy like a meat cleaver."[iv]

Dr. Will B. Palen testified as a witness on behalf of the people: "I am a practicing physician and surgeon in the Village of Walden, have been nearly two years and I made an examination of a body in the rooms of the Twentieth Century Club on the night of September 11th, 1912, in company with Dr. Hadley. I did not know the body at the time, but afterward found it was the body of John Grace."[v]

Dr. Palen's testimony corroborated what Dr. Hadley had said: "A fairly heavy blow would be necessary to break through the skull. Instrument would have to be fairly heavy. The tables of the skull had been broken through. I examined the other parts of the body and they were in physically good condition."[vi]

Helen Grace, Jack's wife, was called on next. She testified that Jack Grace left their home September 7th at 7:00 P.M. and that she never saw him again. He told her he would be back at 11:00 P.M. She stated that when Jack left that he had $20 and $50 bills with him. She did not know how many $50 bills, but she said he had $320 in all. She also testified that when he left their home, he had two diamond rings and a diamond cluster pin on his person. The prosecution presented the jewelry that had been found in the cake of soap in Bill Grace's shaving mug and Helen Grace identified them as belonging to Jack Grace. She also testified that the stone in one of the rings had been hers and that Louis Kades, a jeweler from Newburgh, had reset it in early September. She also told the court that William Grace had come to visit them in Newburgh and that she had heard him and Jack talking about Fannie Andrews. Jack had asked Bill if he was going to marry Fannie. Helen testified that, "He said he was going there for friendship. Jack said if he did intend to marry

The Grace Murder Case

her he would appear and tell he had another wife. Wm. said he did not intend to marry the girl. That was all that was said about the marriage."[vii] Helen also told the court that Jack and Bill had gone to Fall River together from the Wednesday or Thursday before Labor Day and returned on Labor Day.

Jesse Wade was the next witness. He was a blade finisher in the knife works and had seen Jack Grace at the Eagle hotel on Saturday night, September 7th, 1912. It was shortly after eight o'clock and they had drinks together at the Eagle with Elson Ranteh and a man named Christian. He said that Bill Grace was not with them at this time and that he had not seen Bill Grace that night. He told the court that he saw a pin and one ring on Jack Grace. When shown the jewelry, he said that they were very much like what he had seen. Under cross examination, Mr. Wade revealed that he had seen Jack Grace twice that night and that, the first time, Jack had told him he was there to meet an actress friend of his and, the second time he ran into Jack, he had told him that he still had not met with this woman.

Up next was Philip Christian, who may be who Jesse Wade referred to as a man named Christian. He said he had seen both Jack and Bill Grace on the stoop of the Eagle Hotel at eleven o'clock on September 7th. He said he had "walked down the street with him, that is Jack and Bill walked down street far as Terwilliger's Cigar Store. We all went in the Cigar Store. Don't know how long they remained, they stayed out in front. I went in the back room, remained there until after 12 P.M. Neither Will or John Grace was there when I came out. I never saw John Grace again."[viii] He also testified that the ring and cluster pin that the prosecution showed were similar to the ones that Jack Grace was wearing that night.

The transcript says that Charles Corcoran is recalled, but it should read that James Corcoran is re-called. The court clerk, J. D. McGiffert, made many such mistakes in his transcription.

The Trial

Regardless, James testifies that: "I saw John Grace Saturday night, September 7th, 1912 in pool room of Terwilliger's cigar store, and did not see Wm. Grace at that time. I was on the streets of Walden until about three o'clock in the morning and during that time I heard some noise, I was standing in front of Cooper's Drug Store four or five stores up from the Century Club, stood there about 2 o'clock."[ix] He said that somebody hollered "oh" twice. Mr. Bennet objected to this as improper, irrelevant, and immaterial, but he was overruled. James continues, "I was standing on the corner of Main St., after I heard the holler within one door of the Twentieth Century Club, I remained there about one hour. Had been on Main St., ever since 12:00 until I went into the house which was half past three or four o'clock. Did not see Will Grace on Main St., that night between twelve o'clock and the time I went in the house about four."[x]

Orville Thompson, a village police officer, was questioned after Corcoran. The main point of his testimony was that he was on duty the evening of September 8, 1912 walking Main Street with Chief Ronk and Officers Ronk and Lyons until about three o'clock and that he did not see Bill Grace on Main Street or anywhere else. Although the transcript says the evening of the 8th, it means the evening of the 7th and into the morning of September 8th.

Dill Ronk testified after Thompson and confirmed that he was with Chief Ronk and Officer Lyons between the hours of twelve and three-thirty or four o'clock. He said he actually stood on Snyder's stoop, near the Century Club, where you can see the front of the Club, from 3 A.M. to 4 A.M. and at 4 A.M., he used the toilet in Terwilliger's Cigar Store as he had the key. While in the store, he heard someone moving around right over the front part of the building. Under cross examination by Bennet, he said it was customary to hear noises of that kind up

The Grace Murder Case

there at different times and explained that was the reason he did not go up to investigate.

Fred Fox testified at the trial. A resident of the village engaged in the Cutlery business, he knew both of the Grace boys. He said, "I recollect Sunday morning, September 8th. I attempted to go in rooms of Twentieth Century Club about five or ten minutes after six that morning, and was unable to get in. I had a key to the door, tried it, but it would not work."[xi]

"I could not open the door with my key, I just braced against it, tried to push it open, but it would not go."[xii] Had Fox succeeded in securing an entrance, through the door at the top of the stairs, which was found according to a September 14th *Newburgh Daily News* article, to have been nailed shut by the murderer, he might have shared the fate of Jack Grace. There was no mention of the door being nailed shut at the trial.[xiii]

Fox went on to state that he never had any trouble in getting in the same door before. He said he had gone over to the rooms because he was standing in front of the Bank with Eugene Lupton, Mike Deegan, and Frank Hargian, and they heard a noise over in the rooms, like somebody hammering, then they heard somebody moving things around. They looked up and, in a few minutes, saw a rag come up to the window and somebody in shirt sleeves wiping the window off.

The court clerk, besides spelling people's names wrong even within a paragraph, also wrote a lot of summaries rather than a word for word transcription. It is difficult to follow and understand what was actually being said. Eugene's testimony corroborated Fred Fox's story, and because their stories also agreed, neither Mike Deegan nor Frank Harrigan, who had also been with them, were called upon to testify.

Charles Burlison testified soon after Fred and Eugene. He worked in Thos. Terwilliger's Cigar Store and was working there that same Sunday morning. He saw William Grace

The Trial

coming down the stairs from the Twentieth Century Club rooms at a quarter of seven and spoke with him. This was perhaps the most damaging testimony to Bill's case: it places him at the crime scene. Also, the three previous witnesses said they were there at 6:10, so this is just one-half hour later. Charles testified he was sweeping off the sidewalk and when Bill came down the stairs, he asked Bill if he had been sleeping upstairs. Bill replied, "No, I left a bundle up stairs last night, and went up after it this morning." Bill then went into the Cigar store and bought a pack of cigarettes. He pulled out a handkerchief that had blood stains on it and Charles asked him if he had cut his finger. Bill responded that he was subject to nose bleeds. If Bill had really just committed this murder, he was certainly cool, calm, and collected. After he left, he went in the direction of the post office, which would have been on Main Street in the opposite direction of his boarding house. Bill Grace, in his testimony, says this was incorrect and that he went in the direction of his boarding house. The prosecution had a bloody handkerchief at trial, but he could not identify it as the one he saw.[xiv]

After Burlison, it is Harry Crawford's turn on the stand. He was a hotel Clerk at the Eagle Hotel. He testified that he saw both Jack and Bill on September 7th at the Eagle between 8 and 9 P.M. He noticed that Jack wore a cluster pin and identified it as similar to the one shown to him by the prosecution. Under cross examination, Bennett gets Crawford to admit that Jack was with two or three other people when he saw them and that he did not know who they were.[xv]

The original Walden Savings Bank on the corner of Bank and Main Streets. The murder took place in the building that is diagonal to this building. This is where Fred Fox and his friends where standing when they saw someone wiping the windows at the Twentieth Century Club in the early morning hours of September 8, 1912. Postcard courtesy of Lisa Melville.

Louis Kades, the jeweler from Newburgh, was called next to confirm that the ring in the prosecution's possession was the one he reset for John Grace in June of 1912. The diamond was from a lady's ring that he had never seen before. This is damaging testimony because Bill Grace had this ring in his possession and here is a professional confirming that it is Jack's ring. Helen Grace was the only other witness that was able to say for sure that this was Jack's jewelry; the rest could only say that it was similar to what they saw on Jack Grace.[xvi]

The Trial

JEWELRY
SUCH AS YOU WOULD LIKE TO GET

This is a Jewelry Store for everybody, where you can select from the biggest and best assortment of popular and high-priced pieces of

DIAMONDS, JEWELRY, WATCHES and RINGS

All the Latest Designs

LOUIS KADES
Jeweler & Silversmith
33 WATER STREET
H. R. Phone 387-J   NEWBURGH, N. Y.

Louis Kades Advertisement from page 99 of Historic Wallkill and Hudson River Valley magazine, 1913, published by Wallkill Publishing Association, Walden, NY.

Fannie Andrews took the stand next. It must have been extremely hard for Fannie to testify with Bill Grace in the room, but she did. Fannie testifies that she wed William Grace on September 11th, 1912 and went to New York for their honeymoon. She came back on Thursday the 12th of September with two suitcases. One of them was hers and the other was the one that Bill Grace had borrowed from her brother-in-law to use on their trip. She gave the suitcases to Chief Ronk when he came to her house on the 15th. Charles Young was the reporter with Chief Ronk when the suitcases were opened.[xvii]

Inside the suitcase were Grace's clothes and his shaving mug. The rings and pin were found hidden in the cake of soap in the shaving mug. Fannie said that when Grace left her in New

The Grace Murder Case

York on September 12th, he had left her with $150 in $50 bills. She continued that they had gone to New York on Monday and Tuesday of that same week before the wedding and that he had paid all the expenses there. They went to Coney Island. He did not purchase anything for himself, but he did buy her a willow plume for her hat for which he paid $10. She also stressed that she knew him for a year and he did not in that time show her a diamond ring, or pin, nor did she see it when they went to New York, although there is a contradicting sentence that seems out of place and may be the clerk's error again. She says, according to the transcript: "He had one small diamond that is all I know. He never wore this pin or either of those rings."[xviii]

After Fannie is finished, Chief Ronk confirms her story about the suitcases and finding the rings and pin in the soap of the shaving mug. He then describes the night of September 11th for the court:

> I went in Twentieth Century Club where Grace's body was found. There was such a smell there we had to throw stuff around before we could stay in the room. Everything was scattered with blood, the carpet and windows. You could see blood scattered against on of the front windows next to the street, that is Main St., the walls and cushion was all soaked with blood and the cuspidor was half full of blood. The galvanized tin pail was all covered with blood; the covering over the couch where his body was found was soaked with blood. I saw [a] meat cleaver (shown witness) before in [the] Club Room of [the] Twentieth Century Club. It was found in room on west side opposite to side where body was found [sic].[xix]

The Trial

The chief had found the cleaver and testified that it had blood spatters and dark hair on the back, blunt side.

"Bill" Grace's Boarding House Mistress and the Walden Girl Whom He Duped Into Marriage

This sketch of Fannie Andrews appeared in the December 11, 1912 edition of the *Newburgh Daily News*. She is wearing a stylish feather plume. Is it the plume that Bill Grace bought for her before they married? The other woman is Mrs. Fannie Kidd, Bill Grace's landlady at 11 James Street.

The trial transcript is where we learn more about Bill and Jack's life in Walden. Much of the story is supplemented by the newspapers and, although newspapers may not be completely reliable, they add information that may not have been admissible in court. While in Walden, Bill Grace worked as a painter for John Reid. John Reid testified at the trial that Bill had worked for him for about a year and made a total amount somewhere in the neighborhood of $560. He went to work in June of 1911 and worked until August 12th of 1912. He received $13.50 for a full week. He said that Grace would occasionally

67

come to him and ask for a salary advance of one or two dollars, sometimes fifty cents. The reason that he often used was that he was short of money.

Another witness at the trial was Thomas Murphy, the owner of Murphy's bar at the Metropol in Newburgh, where Jack Grace worked as a bartender. Thomas Murphy had a conversation with Bill Grace a few days before Labor Day of 1912. He asked to borrow five dollars so he could travel with his brother Jack to go see their mother. He never repaid the loan. Clinton Hawkins, from Walden, also loaned money to Grace without ever getting it back and testified at the trial. The prosecution was trying to show that Bill was broke and that, after his brother was dead, he was suddenly able to pay off his debts and even bought Fanny a gift and himself a new suit for his wedding.

William Palenthorpe, a tailor in Walden, testified that, in the latter part of August 1912, Grace ordered a suit of clothes for himself at a cost of $24.50. Bill Grace paid for it on September 10th, on the day he was married, before the ceremony was performed. Later that day, his brother's lifeless body was found.

Mr. Palenthorpe said it was the first suit of clothes Bill had bought from him. In early September, he sold him a shirt for $1.50. He did not pay for it then, but paid all his debt on September 10th.

After Palenthorpe testified, it was Fanny Kidd's turn. Fanny was Bill's landlady; she owned the boarding house at 11 James Street in Walden. She told the court that Bill Grace had boarded with her for a year and that "on or about" September 10th, he owed her $10 for two weeks board. He had told her that he could not pay her until he returned from his trip to Fall River with Jack to see their mother on Labor Day weekend. Bill told Mrs. Kidd that he did not have the money and did not want to go home with "nothing." He did pay his $10 debt to Fanny Kidd

The Trial

on Sunday morning, September 8th, the morning after Jack Grace was allegedly killed.

There does seem to be a lot of evidence that Bill Grace was just scraping by before his brother's demise and, after it, he had money to spend. Jack Grace seemed to have been doing much better financially than his little brother.

Mrs. Kidd was also a witness for the defense and Bennett, in cross examination, only asked her if she would be testifying for Bill later. The prosecution also asked her about the things which Bill Grace asked to burn in her back yard, but she did not know what it was that he burned.

William Moore was recalled after Fanny Kidd was done testifying. He was shown the diamond ring and said, "I saw this ring in the village of Walden about September 16th 1912, in the possession of Chief Ronk and examined it closely at that time. I used my glass over it and discovered what I thought was blood."[xx]

Bennett objected to this and it was struck from the record and was changed from "and discovered what I thought to be blood." to "I saw a discoloration or some red color on the ring down in the setting."[xxi]

Ronk was also called regarding the discoloration that was underneath the diamond. He said he saw the red color as well. This is when Talcott C. Vanamee was called. Dr. Vanamee was a practicing physician in the City of Newburgh; he had six to eight months of experience testing blood in the "Laboratory, Post Graduate Hospital, New York City." He said that he had examined the diamond the morning of the first day of the trial. He determined that the red had all the external earmarks of a clot of blood and then he took it off and examined it under a microscope. At this point in the testimony, the judge asked Mr. Wilson if he intended to have the doctor examine the handkerchief as well and Wilson said yes, so the court had it

The Grace Murder Case

marked for identification and it was examined. Under cross examination (again the clerk is missing a lot here), Vanamee said some of the stains on the handkerchief are blood. Vanamee said in all probability it was human blood, but he would not swear to it.

Vanamee took a long time explaining the tests he had performed; however, it is obvious that this science was not something the lawyers or many people of the day were too familiar with. The clerk's records are not very clear and this testimony ended quickly and did not seem to prove anything other than that there was mammal blood on the ring.

After Dr. Vanamee, Mrs. Kidd was recalled. She said that Bill Grace had two suitcases which he no longer wanted and told her to give them away to a junk man. She gave them to Officer Lyons the Sunday after Grace's marriage. He brought the suitcases to Ronk who opened them in front of Mr. Moore and found the handkerchief which was marked for identification.

The handkerchief was not identified as being bloody; it just said it was marked for identification. They may have been trying to show that this handkerchief and the bloody handkerchief were both Grace's. It seems they were also trying to clarify which suitcases Grace borrowed for his honeymoon trip and which ones were his old ones that he got rid of before his wedding. He used Fannie's brother-in-law's suitcase for the honeymoon and that is the suitcase where Jack's jewelry was found in the cake of soap in the shaving mug. Fannie Andrews was briefly called to confirm that the suitcase she gave to Ronk is the one that Bill had on their honeymoon. After this, the people rested.

Bennett opened with a formal motion that the Court direct a verdict of acquittal. It was denied. Then, the Court asked Wilson if there was any money found on the dead man and

The Trial

Wilson said there was no evidence as to that. The Court continued that it is very important that it be shown that he had $300 when he left Newburgh. Chief George Ronk was recalled to testify and he confirmed that when they searched all of John Grace's pockets, they only found twenty-one cents. Then, the people rested again, reserving the right to call Officer Lyons.

Mr. Bennett opened the case for the defendant by calling the first of several character witnesses. He first called Floyd Olvia who was a member of the Twentieth Century Club. Floyd stated that Bill Grace generally had a good character and that he had not heard anything derogatory about him before the murder happened. He was followed by Edmond Oliva and Jimmy Haly who both confirmed the same thing. Joe Litson, also a member of the Twentieth Century Club, was called by Bennett to show that Grace did indeed play poker and sometimes won money. When Litson was cross-examined however, he admitted that Bill Grace borrowed money from him three or four times, but he never borrowed over two dollars.

Charles Dimsuth was called just to confirm that another person had played poker with Bill Grace at the Club. William Dewitt and Fred Seeger testified that they would often see Grace at the Club. Mr. Seeger added that he often saw Bill Grace leaving the Club rooms on Sunday mornings, having slept there overnight.

George Ronk was recalled on behalf of the defense. Bennett asked him about a conversation he had with Bill Grace on the night of September 10th; the prosecution objected but it was overruled. However, Ronk was only allowed to answer yes or no as to whether or not he had a conversation with Bill Grace. He was not allowed to say what was said in the conversation, so whatever Grace's lawyer wanted to reveal about the conversation was thwarted.

The Grace Murder Case

Will Hunt, a painter and Bill Grace's foreman at his painting job, was asked if he remembered Grace showing him a roll of money, but he testified that he did not remember Grace ever showing him a roll of money. When pressed for an answer, he said that Grace did show him money, but only in small amounts.

The defense then recalled Fanny Andrews. She was asked if Bill had showed her a roll of money and she did not recall that he did, but she said "he always had plenty to go around any place."[xxii] She was again asked specifically if he showed her money known as yellow backs or money of large denominations at the moving picture show at Newburgh. She did not remember any such occasion.

William Palenthorpe, the tailor, was then recalled and asked if he remembered when Grace came in to have his suit made and if he offered to pay for it at that time. Palenthorpe said Grace had offered to pay at that time, but that he did not pay. The transcript does not explain this any further.

Fanny Kidd, Grace's landlady, was also recalled and said, "I found him a very honest young man respectfully to my elderly husband and myself [sic]."[xxiii] This sentence was objected to by the prosecution and was struck from the record.

Walden Police officer Frank Lyons testified that, on September 15th, he went over to Fannie Kidd's boarding house and picked up two suitcases that belonged to William Grace. He took them to Chief Ronk that afternoon and they opened them together. But there is nothing else said about these suitcases, so it is unclear why Bennett called this witness. It almost appears like the clerk is being even less precise with recording the defendant's case than he was with the prosecution.

. Jesse Wade was the last witness called for the defense before Bill Grace took the stand himself. Mr. Wade told the court that

The Trial

he saw Jack Grace that night for the first time at the Lincoln Hotel (he most likely said the Eagle Hotel) and had a drink with him. Jack told Jesse he could not stay long because his brother told him to come to Walden to meet his actress friend who had in the neighborhood of four to five hundred dollars to spend.

Then, Anthony William Grace took the stand. This was a pivotal move for his case. How he came across to the jury would mean his life or death. Grace admitted that he married Fannie Andrews on September 11, 1912 and went to the city on his honeymoon where he learned of his brother's death. He explained how he heard of the death and his trip back to Walden. As soon as he got back to Walden, he was brought to the inquest being held in Colonel Bradley's office. He was subsequently indicted.

He goes on to explain how he earned and was also given some of the $370 he had the day he was married. He details what happened the night of September 7, 1912. He was asked whether he had phoned his brother on the 5th to tell him to come to Walden to meet the actress. The prosecution wanted to know because this would show premeditation of the murder, but Jack came to Walden on Saturday, September 7th. There seems to be some confusion on what happened on which date, but it could also be the recording of the information. Bill Grace testified that he saw his brother that Sunday night. Bill said he was going up to Dominie Sizoo's house when he met Jack on the corner of Orchard Street and Main. He said Jack gave him the diamonds to look after for a while because they had gotten him into trouble the night before. He said that when he heard of his brother's death the first thing he thought of was: "Good God, if they found these on me they would swear I killed my brother"[xxiv] so he hid them in the shaving mug. Would this be the first thought of someone who had just found out his beloved brother was dead?

The Grace Murder Case

Bill then said he went to the city with Fannie Andrews that Monday and was married on Wednesday. He said that on Sunday morning, he went to the club to see if there was a poker game going on. Bill said he had gone to the club at five o'clock, but could not get in until he returned around seven. It's then that he remembered the bundle he left there: it was a shirt and two collars and they are now in his trunk in his prison cell. He said he saw Mr. Burlison a little after seven o'clock when he got around the corner of the building. Mr. Burlison said he saw Grace coming down the stairs and into the cigar store to buy a smoke. Bill Grace corrects himself and says when he came downstairs the second time, he found Burlison standing in the doorway of the tobacco store.

Bill Grace then testified that he saw his brother with a girl on Saturday, September 7th, at a little after twelve o'clock, which would make it September 8th; he said he had seen the girl with him before. He claims to have seen him last on Sunday night, September 8th and, at that time, he was alone. Later, he testifies that a man named O'Conner or O'Connel was with his brother when he saw him on Sunday morning and that he did not mention it here because he was not asked about that.

He claims that he and Jack Grace and two girls were on Church Hill until about 1 A.M. Sunday morning. He said that Jack Grace left him with a woman named Nell. He said that the other girl's name was Bess, the one that went with Jack, and that he did not know whether she was the actress that he had told his brother about that was coming to Walden. This seems really odd that he would not recognize for sure whether it was the actress that lured Jack to Walden. He said he left Nell in front of the Terrace Inn, about 3:15 A.M. and that he did not know if she went in the Terrace Inn or not. She did not tell him where she was going; only that she was going to wait on the stoop for her friend. Then, Bill Grace said he went home.

The Trial

After this questioning, Bill is asked about his marriages. He admitted to marrying Annie Jones, Jennie Schiegler, and Fannie Andrews, and that he knew that he was a bigamist.

He is then asked why he lied about his mother's death. He told the court that his brother told him to do it. He testified that Jack never told him why he wanted him to tell everyone that his mother was dead, but that he did it. He admitted that he was lying about it, but added that he was not under oath when he told the coroner that she was dead.

He said that he continued with the lie about his mother being dead after his brother's death because "I felt foolish to think I had lied before."[xxv] He then clarified that he did not go all the way to Fall River with his brother on their Labor Day weekend trip; he, instead, had remained in Newport because he knew that his first wife was in Fall River. He also told the court that his brother did not pay the expenses for their trip and that there was no trouble between them. He also confirms that his brother was married at Fall River, Massachusetts and was also a bigamist.

He stressed that he did not tell anyone that his brother left him that Saturday night at 11:00 or 11:15, the last night Jack Grace was seen by anyone other than Bill Grace. He told the court that his brother left him at a little after 1:00 and that he stayed in front of the church until 3:00 or a little later waiting for him, and then went to his boarding house.

Grace is then cross examined about the women that were there with him and his brother. He only knew the woman with him as Nell and her friend was Bess. He didn't know whether she was the actress. It was, however, the woman he had phoned his brother about on September 5th; he had met the girls on September 4th at 12:30 P.M. He did not know their last names, where they were living, or how long they had been in Walden. He did not know if they worked.

Sketch from December 11, 1912 edition of the Newburgh Daily News. The heading reads: "Apathetic Pose of Grace on Witness Stand and Other Pen pictures Made During the Trail by News Artist Gillett."

He reiterated that he had left Nell in front of the Terrace Inn at 3:15 A.M. and then, he went home and sat on the stoop until about five o'clock. Then, he went up Main Street and saw other people, but didn't know any of them. He saw Dill Ronk sitting in front of the Saint Nicholas Hotel. He tried the door at the Twentieth Century Club, but could not get in, so walked across the Kills (the Wallkill River) and kept walking until seven

The Trial

o'clock, but his watch had stopped, so he was not sure of the time. He tried the door again and got in. He did not think about why he couldn't get in at five o'clock, but could get in at seven o'clock. This was when he ran into Charles Burlison as he swept off the sidewalk in front of the cigar store.

Bill Grace is next questioned about his finances. He talks about making $13.50 a week as a painter for Mr. Reed and agreed with Mr. Reed's testimony of making $560 while working for him. He paid $5 a week to Mrs. Kidd for board and was there for 52 weeks, costing $260. He explained that he had other income from gambling and claimed he played with Mr. Didsbury, the owner of the local theater, who had denied playing with him. He said the largest winning he ever made was $18 and the most he lost was $4. He said he saved $185 dollars from playing poker in the little more than a year he lived in Walden.

Terrace Inn in Walden, New York. Postcard courtesy of Marcus Millspaugh.

The Grace Murder Case

The Orange County Press, December 13, 1912 edition, in describing Bill Grace's testimony says: "'Five and ten cent,' said Grace. There was a smile of incredulity on the faces of many men in the court room as the absurd statement was made. A man would have about as much chance of winning several hundred dollars in a five and ten cent limit poker game as he would of boring his way through the antipodes with a darning needle."[xxvi]

Picture of Newburgh Courthouse before its renovation and reuse. This is how it would have looked during Bill Grace's trial. Photograph courtesy of City of Newburgh Historian's office. City of Newburgh Historian Mary McTamaney.

Boring his way through the Antipodes with a darning needle? This was 1912 and language has changed a little and this saying is not as common today. The Antipodes of any place

78

The Trial

on the Earth is the place that is diametrically opposite it. Today, a more common expression might be: "digging his way to China."

He also tells the court that he would write to his mother to send him money and that inside of a year she had sent him $400. He admits to asking for money from his mother even though he had his own money. He claims that he had $376 he kept in his room at the Kidd's boarding house. He would save up small bills and then ask his brother to exchange it for large ones because he was less likely to break a large bill than a small one.

Mr. Grace is cross examined and for the next ten pages of transcript, the same things that were in previous testimonies were revisited. It seems very repetitive and nothing new really surfaces. Then, the defense rested. There were no closing remarks, but Wilton Bennett had many charge requests of his own for the jury after Judge Tompkins charged the all male jury to deliberate Bill Grace's fate.

> Miss Andrews, who had listened to all the testimony with a calm demeanor, grew nervous while the jury was out. When the foreman knocked on the door, the sharp rat-tat was too much for her frayed nerves, and she gave a start and a scream. As the minutes passed and Justice Thompkins failed to appear, the suspense became too much for the girl and she also gave way to tears. She was led down to the room in which sat the first matrimonial victim of the convicted fratricide [sic], and while the man who had deceived them both was receiving a sentence of death in the room overhead, the two women sat with bowed heads, each trying to console the other.[xxvii]

Newspapers say the jury deliberated only a few minutes, but the trial transcript indicates they retired to the jury room at 3:45 P.M. and that they returned at 4:40 P.M., so they actually deliberated for close to an hour before coming back with a guilty verdict.

Antone waived his option to wait two days before hearing his punishment and the sentence was pronounced: "William Grace, the sentence of the Court is that you be delivered into the custody of the keeper of Sing Sing State Prison, and that during the week commencing January 27th, 1913, you be put to death in the manner prescribed by law."[xxviii]

Helen Grace, the woman who claimed she was the legal widow of John Grace, the murdered man, maintained her composure throughout the entire afternoon. When Grace was sentenced to die according to law, she looked at him and smiled.

Although Mrs. Annie Grace was not in the court room when the jury reported its verdict and Grace was sentenced to die, she visited him in his cell the night before at about 6 P.M. She did not say much then, but promised to visit him the next morning. Immediately after he had eaten his breakfast, he asked if Annie Grace had been there yet. When he was told that she had not, he asked that she be phoned. They called the Dell House where she was staying and were told that she was on her way.

"When Mrs. Grace was admitted to the cell she burst into tears and threw her arms around Grace's neck. For a few minutes she could not say a word, but just sobbed and cried unrestrainedly. During the scene Grace patted her on the back and murmured terms of endearment in her ear. The jailers, hardened as they are to all kinds of human misery, were moved to tears by the sorrow and grief shown by the Massachusetts woman."[xxix]

On December 19, 1912, Wilton Bennett filed an appeal on behalf of his client, Anthony William Grace. The appeal failed

The Trial

and so did Grace's attempt at getting clemency from Governor William Sulzer. Bill Grace was again sentenced to die on August 4, 1913.

"William Anthony Grace, Convicted of the Murder of his Own Brother in Cold Blood, Hears His Death Sentence Pronounced Without a Tremor." Sketch from the December 12, 1912 *Newburgh Daily News*.

81

The Grace Murder Case

The Palentine Hotel was across the street from the Newburgh courthouse and was where jurors and the rest of court lunched at breaks during the trial. It has been demolished and the site is now home to the Newburgh Public Library. Postcard courtesy of Newburgh Historical Society.

There is one article that indicates Bill Grace was emotional about the verdict. It is in the Thursday, December 12, 1912 edition of the Port Jervis Evening Gazette that says:

> William Anthony Grace, who was sentenced to be put to death at Sing Sing Prison during the last week in January for the murder of his brother, "Jack" Grace, the wrestler, at Walden, last September, attempted to end his life at the jail in Newburgh Tuesday night by smothering himself with his pillow and blanket. His effort was foiled by jail attendants, who discovered him after he had become unconscious, and resuscitated him. The prison authorities delivered Grace at Sing Sing Prison Wednesday afternoon.

The Trial

Before leaving Grace inquired if a confession would save him from the electric chair. His wife from Fall River, Mass., whom he deserted and later married two other women, called on him Wednesday and pledged him her co-operation to obtain a new trial or a commutation of the death sentence to imprisonment for life.

The Grace Murder Case

[i] *Orange County Times- Press*, December 13, 1912, p.1
[ii] Court Transcript, p. 28
[iii] Court Transcript, p.8
[iv] Court Transcript, p.8
[v] Court Transcript, p. 29
[vi] Court Transcript, p. 29
[vii] Court Transcript, p. 32
[viii] Court Transcript, p.36
[ix] Court Transcript, p. 37
[x] Court Transcript, p. 38
[xi] Court Transcript, p. 40
[xii] Court Transcript, p. 40
[xiii] *Newburgh Daily News,* September 14, 1912, p.1
[xiv] Court Transcript, p. 43
[xv] Court Transcript, p. 45
[xvi] Court Transcript, p. 45
[xvii] Court Transcript, p. 46
[xviii] Court Transcript, p. 48
[xix] Court Transcript, p.50
[xx] Court Transcript, p. 57
[xxi] Court Transcript, p. 57
[xxii] Court Transcript, p.70)
[xxiii] Court Transcript, p. 71
[xxiv] Court Transcript, p. 75
[xxv] Court Transcript, p. 78
[xxvi] *The Orange County Press,* December 13, 1912, p.1
[xxvii] *Newburgh Daily News,* December 11, 1912. p.1
[xxviii] Court Transcript, p. 130
[xxix] *Newburgh Daily News,* December 11, 1912, p.1

4

THE OTHER VICTIMS

In spite of what happened, Bill's first and only legal wife seems to have stuck by him during his trial. The December 11, 1912 front page of the *Newburgh Daily News* says, "Mrs. Annie Grace still loves Tony."[i] The article says:

> Mrs. Grace said yesterday afternoon, just before she was overcome by hysteria and had to be led from the court room, that Tony was a good boy and a good husband, when he was not under Jack's influence. She said the first few months of their married life had been very happy, but then Jack butted in and enticed her husband to go off with other women. With tears in her eyes, Mrs. Grace said that Tony was not bad at heart but that he was weak and easily led. She said he idolized his brother and used to be happy in the latter's company. She declared that Tony never let her lack for anything when Jack was away from him, but whenever Jack was in the same town, Tony would spend his time drinking and carousing with other women.
>
> "We had a nice home, comfortably furnished and Tony worked steadily and turned his wages over to me. We dressed nicely, lived well and were happy. He seemed to like to spend his spare time with me and not to care for other company."[ii]
>
> "Then Jack came to town and everything changed. Three months before our first baby was born, Tony went away and I had to go out to work to earn money to pay

for my living. He came back shortly after the baby was born and we had a few more months of happiness. Then Jack came to town again and the two went to Lowell. What took place there I do not know, but I understand Tony married a girl under pressure by Jack."[iii]

"Before my second baby was born I had to work and I also had to work the two months preceding the births of our third and fourth children (according to all the other articles they only had 3 children so the paper was possibly embellishing the story a bit). Tony came back, but he did not stay more than three or four weeks. Jack came to town and Tony was out very late with him one night. The next morning Tony told me he would not be back to lunch. I never saw him again until I came to Newburgh and saw him behind the bars charged with murdering Jack."[iv]

While these articles are very enticing and the only recorded sayings of Annie Grace, they must all be taken with a grain of salt. The information was being relayed by telegraph and many of the stories have parts that are incorrect.

The article continues: "I loved Tony when I married him. I love him still. I think he would have been a good husband and devoted father if he had not been under the influence of his brother. For the sake of our children, for the sake of the love I have for him, for his own sake and for my sake, I am going to be his friend now when he needs me."[v]

Annie Grace's willingness to make excuses for her husband's behavior, despite overwhelming evidence to the contrary, shows she is still mesmerized and fooled by him, if this article is to be believed. This really fits into the traits of sociopaths, who can be quite charming. This poor woman really believes that Tony would never hurt her; it was always someone

The Other Victims

else's fault. She blames Jack Grace for her husband's behavior, not recognizing him as one of Bill's victims. After Bill's execution, she shows up in the census in Bill Grace's mother's home for a while with her children and then the trail of what happened to her goes cold. A single mother of three in 1913 would most likely need to remarry to have any financial security, since job opportunities that paid a living wage to women were so limited.

Annie Grace had said she did not know what Bill had done in Lowell, Massachusetts. She was not aware that he had married Jennie Shrigley under the name of Arthur Brooks. Before Jennie gave birth to a son, Bill deserted her, taking some funds which belonged to Jennie's brother-in-law, John Livesey. No divorce was secured from his first wife, so this marriage was not legal.

In 1911, Mrs. Jennie Shrigley Brooks is listed in a local Lowell directory at 88 Andrews Street, Lowell, Massachusetts. Sarah Jane Shrigly (Jennie) was the daughter of Edward and Elizabeth J. (Mather) Shrigley. She was born in Tewksbury, Massachusetts. In the September 14, 1912 edition of the *Fall River Daily Globe*, Jennie is described as a handsome, young woman. She and Arthur William Brooks were married in the Sacred Heart Church rectory in Lowell on October 19, 1910 by Father Fletcher. Brooks (Bill Grace) had become a partner in a grocery business of his new brother-in-law and the firm name was Livesey & Brooks. He had met Jennie at her boarding house on Lawrence Street while he was working at the Lowell Bleachery Company. At the Lowell Bleachery, he was said to have been known under the names of Brooks, Waddington, and Rivers. He had also frequently told his acquaintances that his mother died recently in Fall River and that when he was twenty-five years old, he would inherit $40,000.[vi] It seems that Mr.

The Grace Murder Case

Grace liked to create incredible stories about himself and had lied about his mother's death before he did so in Walden.

The son that Jennie had by Grace was either put up for adoption or died because he does not show up in any of her records, although one reference was made that he was with Jennie's mother. Life continued to be hard for Jennie after she was abandoned by Grace and found out the truth about him. She married William H. Keeler between 1912 and 1915. They had two daughters: Vivian in 1913 and Eileen Keeler in 1915. They also had one son, William Russel Keeler, who died at the age of eleven months on May 4, 1917. William H. Keeler died in 1918 at the age of 27. His obituary says he died at the contagious hospital, so he may have been a victim of the 1918 flu epidemic. In the 1920 census, Jennie Keeler is boarding in Westford and working at a mill. Vivian and Eileen Keeler are in St. Peter's Orphanage in Lowell. She soon married Fred Stewart and was able to get her daughters back. It's during this marriage that lasts until Fred's death in 1944 that Jennie finally seems to get some long-term security. Again, this was a time when a woman's reputation was all she had, and to not be legally married and have given birth in this time period would have been extremely difficult.

The murder investigation uncovered Bill Grace's two previous wives. Some articles in the *Fall River Daily Globe* hint that there may have been more. Neither Annie nor Jennie testified at Grace's trial; only Fannie Andrew's testified. Annie attended the trial, but Jennie did not. It was decided that all that needed to be established for the trial was that he was a bigamist and that was established when Annie went to Walden and swore that Bill Grace was in fact her husband, Antone William Grace. Both women were spared from having to testify. Fannie Andrews was not so lucky and needed to testify about the days in September that she shared with Bill Grace.

The Other Victims

Fannie Andrews was born in Walden on September 8, 1887. She was the daughter of William B. and Annie Lockwood Andrews. She had one brother, Leighton, and one sister named Edith. The 1878-79 *Orange County Directory* lists two Wm. Andrews residing in Walden and lists them both as cutlers. This would make sense since most of the town was involved in the knife industry in some way. William B. Andrews, Fannie's father, died on January 22, 1889, when she was two years old. I am sure that this had a tremendous impact on the family. It is probably why her mother ran their house as a boarding house. This was one of the only acceptable money-making opportunities available to older women.

The night before she married for the second time, you can bet that Bill Grace crossed Fannie Andrews' mind, even if it was just the contrast in the situation. On July 2, 1918, when she was 31 years old, she married Herbert Mason who was 39. They continued to live in Walden until their deaths in the 1960s. Her marriage to Mason lasted 43 years and, by all accounts, she was very happy with Herb. Herb was a cutler who worked in the Schrade Knife Company. It was nice to learn that after such an unpleasant experience, she stayed in Walden, was happily married, and was an active member of the Saint Andrews Episcopal Church, which was a short walk from her house on Orchard Street. The house at 28 Orchard Street where she lived the rest of her life was torn down and is now the site of a municipal parking lot. When her mother died, she inherited the house along with her sister and brother. Fannie's brother, Leighton, and his wife lived in one half and Fannie and Herb lived in the other half. It is not clear if they lived in the house while Fannie's mother was still alive, for she lived 29 years after Herb and Fannie married.

I interviewed Fannie's great niece at her Walden home on April 3, 2004. Her relationship was through her mother's aunt

The Grace Murder Case

through Herb Mason, Fannie's second husband. She was only a child when she knew Fannie, but said Fannie loved children even though she never had any of her own. Fannie would give her goodies when she went to visit and was a very nice lady. She said Fannie and Herb were quiet and kept to themselves for the most part.

Fannie's great niece said there had been a falling out between Leighton and Herb, and Fannie, being a dutiful wife, respected her husband's wishes and was not close to her brother anymore. It seems to indicate that perhaps Herb was a bit stubborn. After all, Leighton is mentioned in the newspaper articles about the murder case as trying to protect and help his little sister. To be fair, we cannot know who the stubborn party was since we do not know what the argument was about.

Fannie will always be a bit of a mystery because she never wrote or talked about the incident as far as anyone knows. I have found people who knew her when she was older. She lived until 1964, but all they remembered was that she was plump, but a very lovely, pleasant, and proper woman. They all sort of knew something had happened, but no one ever pressed her about it and she did not volunteer to talk about it. Also, most of those still around who knew her were children or very young adults when she was an old woman, so they did not remember many specifics about her and the gossip about the Grace Murder had lessened over time.

Without any firsthand knowledge, I have speculated what it must have been like for Fannie with help from newspaper articles from the time. I felt sympathy for Fannie that went beyond the nearly hundred years since her heart break and the fantastic story behind it. She was a young woman when it happened, twenty-five years old.

When Fanny heard the news that her husband had been arrested for the murder and that he was a bigamist, she

The Other Victims

screamed that she did not believe them. She demanded they take her to him; she wanted to hear it from him that he was already married.

The shock was setting in; the pain of betrayal was like a knife cutting through skin and then a slow ache that did not seem to go away. She did not want to believe it. How could it be true? This was her Bill; her best friend, her lover, her love. He would not have lied to her, would he?

It slowly sank in that if he was already married, then his marriage to her was not legal. He had used her; he was a liar, and a betrayer, but was he capable of murder?

As she began to recover from the initial shock, she began to get angry. She did not know this man. For a year, they had shared their lives, talking, joking, sharing meals, family functions, kissing, holding hands, and she trusted him completely. She loved him; she wanted to be his wife and to grow old with him. Her family accepted him and was happy for her. Now, she felt ashamed, stupid, and embarrassed that she did not suspect anything. Her romantic notions of happy ever after were ripped from her young body. Her desire for a family and happy marriage were gone. The feelings of loss were overwhelming. The desire – the need for it to be a different way, for it to be untrue, made it hard to keep believing that this was her reality. It was too much.

She filed for annulment immediately, needing to act, needing to do something to keep this hurt away. Bill, caught in his lie, would not talk to her. He did not know what to say. This only increased her pain. She was beginning to know that this was a life altering event. This was one of those life experiences that would become part of her being, for better or worse. It would make her stronger, but the innocence of youth was gone. The reality of how cruel a person could be was real; it would make her more suspicious of people in general and would cause her

The Grace Murder Case

great distress in trying to trust a man in the future. It would be difficult to trust anyone again.

Her mother, brother, and sister tried to be supportive, but it was 1912: folks did not talk about relationships or sex and this was sordid. This was about bigamy and murder.

The *Orange County Times-Press*, Tuesday September 17, 1912, edition says: "The condition tonight of the bride is such that Dr. F.A. Hadley fears her reason may become affected. She returned from her interrupted honeymoon in response to a message late last night. As soon as she saw her brother Leighton Andrews, she asked: "Where is Bill?"[vii]

"She was put to bed, and it was only this afternoon that her relatives could muster courage to tell her the truth. She then fainted. Later she became hysterical and the family physician was called."[viii]

It is amazing to me that such a "big" story in such a small, very conservative village got lost. I imagine there was a great deal of embarrassment and shame on Fannie's part. Even though the newspaper accounts clearly showed sympathy for the "young innocent girl," there must have been gossip. The damage that gossip causes does not discriminate the innocent from the guilty. It was probably something that lessened and seemed like a forgotten nightmare as the years went by, and that was just the way things were. If you did not talk about them, it was almost as if they never happened. Some things never change. Almost one hundred years later and people still think if they do not talk about something, it might go away, and people still judge each other and gossip. That is actually what is so interesting about people: all these technologies change, fashions, social issues, etc., but the people are very much the same. They all like to think that they are different, but they really are not.

The Other Victims

Women in 1912 could not vote. In all the court proceedings, Fannie is referred to as "the girl." The jury was all male as women were not allowed to serve on juries. There were a few women attorneys, but law was still predominately a male profession until the 1970s. Fannie went to the trial: she not only testified, but she stayed for the trial.

Many of the newspaper accounts were in conflict with each other. As with the headline "Fannie Andrews Prostrated," meaning she was hysterical. Then, in an article a few days later, "Fannie Andrews not Prostrated ...False Rumors of Condition of 'Bill' Grace's Third Wife." There are also stories in the Fall River paper where the first wives of both Jack and Bill Grace are using the papers as a way to get their stories out. It seems that women had to be concerned about gossip and their reputations. A woman's life was determined by how well she married in 1912, and, in some circles, who you marry is still quite important to your quality of life.

Annie Jones, Jennie Shrigly, and Fannie Andrews were all victims of Bill Grace. Their lives were permanently altered by their relationships with him. He left broken hearts, innocent children, and shattered lives behind.

[i] *Newburgh Daily News,* December 11, 1912, p.1
[ii] *Newburgh Daily News,* December 11, 1912, p.1
[iii] *Newburgh Daily News,* December 11, 1912, p.1
[iv] *Newburgh Daily News,* December 11, 1912, p.1
[v] *Newburgh Daily News,* December 11, 1912, p.1
[vi] *Fall River Daily Globe,* September 14, 1912
[vii] *Orange County Times-Press,* September 17, 1912
[viii] *Orange County Times-Press,* September 17, 1912

5

THE EXECUTION

Witnesses to the execution were Dr. T.J. Burke, Detective Moore of Newburgh, Chief Ronk of the Walden Police, and Charles B. Young from the *Newburgh Daily News*. They were served a light luncheon with the Warden and then escorted to the death house. The only other witnesses were two newspaper men and the doctor who was to perform the autopsy. Witnesses sat directly in front of the electric chair.

Grace entered the death chamber at 5:53 P.M. and was pronounced dead at 5:58 P.M. He had lost nearly fifty pounds since his confinement. The night before his death, his attendants said he paced the cell all night. "The change that had taken place in the prisoner impressed those present that he had made a confession. This was neither affirmed nor denied by Father Cashin who attended the doomed man."[i]

Grace never took his eyes from the crucifix and exactly ninety seconds after entering the room, just after he had completed his prayer asking the Divine Being to "forgive me for all my sins," his form strained forward as if it would break the straps.

The first shock given, lasting for one minute, was of 1,960 volts, 40 volts stronger than had ever before been applied to a human being at a similar execution. Following this shock, varying from 9½ to 12 amperes, the physicians examined the body and at 5:57 P.M. another shock of five seconds duration was applied, after which the physicians, including Dr. Burke, with the aid of a stethoscope again examined the victim. At 5:58 P.M., five minutes after entering the death chamber, Bill Grace

The Grace Murder Case

was pronounced dead and the murder of Jack Grace had been avenged in accordance with the laws of the State of New York.

The body was removed to the operating room where an autopsy was performed at which Dr. Burke was again asked to assist. The result of the autopsy disclosed nothing unusual. One witness present, a newspaper man who had witnessed the execution of death sentences by electrocution or hanging on a number of occasions, stated that the electrocution of Grace was the most successful on record.

None of the murderer's family had arranged to claim the body, but previous to his walk to the chair, Grace told Father Cashin that his mother would send for his remains. Father Cashin, when asked about the confession, refused to either affirm or deny it. It is believed, however, by those who have watched other prisoners electrocuted, that his prayer may be regarded as his public confession.[ii]

It seems like they are a little worried here that he did not make a public confession, maybe to assuage any guilt they had to believe that he confessed his crime. Since no one claimed his body, he would have been buried in the Sing Sing cemetery, which was later exhumed and the bodies placed in local cemeteries. This was done to make room for expansions at the prison. It is unlikely that the graves had markers and that they were identified in their new resting places either. The Ossining Historical Society was unable to find out what happened to Bill Grace's body.

Grace had been granted an interview with a newspaper before his execution. In it, Grace said:

> I was –I am–a bigamist. I admit that. I was a bigamist when I married Miss Andrews in New York City on September 11, two days after I was supposed to have killed my brother. But a bigamist is not a murderer, and

The Execution

I am not one. I did not kill my brother, and if the State puts me to death on Monday the State will be killing an innocent man [sic].

These are the facts in my case: I did not know when, where or how my brother was killed until I heard of it at the trial. He and I were very close, had always been so. We were together in Walden on Saturday, September 7, two days before his death. We had an appointment with two girls and we were with them until 1:30 o'clock Sunday morning in the Church Hill Hotel. He went away at that time and I went home. The next morning I inquired about him but could not learn where he had gone. I met him Sunday night with a fellow named O'Conner or O'Connell in Walden. He handed me a long envelope to take care of it for him until he would see me again.

The envelope contained two rings and a stickpin, comparatively worthless. These were part of the evidence used against me at the trial. Is it likely that a murderer would have stopped to steal six cents' worth of jewelry?

On Monday, September 9 I went to the club in the morning to see if there was a poker game going on, and I saw my brother there. I had bought a new shirt and I put it in on in the club. I came out carrying a bundle of laundry. This was also used against me the trial. That afternoon I went to New York with Miss Andrews and returned Tuesday, I asked about my brother, but did not learn where he was. On Wednesday Miss Andrews and I went again to New York and were married in the afternoon.

At midnight in Hotel St. Denis somebody called me up from Newburgh and asked me if I knew my brother had been murdered. I thought somebody was playing a honeymoon joke on us, and answered that of course I did. They asked me if I would come back at once, and I said certainly. I was in such a hurry to get back that I spent $4 for a taxicab in order to make a train.

I was too poor to hire a lawyer and the court appointed one. I knew nothing about law, but I knew I was innocent and never supposed I could be convicted. I did not realize what was happening until the jury was brought in its verdict. That is all I know about the case, and so help me, Heaven, I will go to the chair Monday with the same declaration.

When I wrote to the governor my first letter I was almost sorry to bother him with it, because he has so much trouble. But I did think that I would be able to convince him of my sincerity. I have written again in the hope that perhaps the truth will carry its own persuasion and induce him to give me a hearing. If I could only get to him I know I could convince him of my innocence.[iii]

The same article talks about how the new Warden of Sing Sing, Warden Clancy, had almost been convinced by Bill Grace of his innocence. Clancy did not stay long at Sing Sing: a little later in 1913, he was gone. While Clancy was there, he tried to improve conditions for the prisoners. On Columbus Day in 1912, Warden Clancy made a dramatic innovation, allowing the prisoners to remain out of their cells for a whole day. The following year, Clancy brightened weekends (always dreaded by inmates who were confined in their cramped cells from noon on Saturday to Monday morning) by permitting inmates to remain out in the open air on Sunday morning.

The lockstep had been abolished in 1900 by order of Superintendent of Prisons Collins and, in 1904, the striped

The Execution

uniform was abandoned as a "badge of disgrace."[iv] The rule of silence was abandoned about 1914, after Bill Grace's stay there. Prisoners had not been allowed to talk or communicate with each other in any way whatsoever. The prisoners ate in silence, worked in silence, and existed in a quiet world where penitence was the goal. They walked together in lock step, in their striped prison uniforms, like robots, one behind another.

This sketch of Antone William Grace appeared in the August 4, 1913 edition of the *Newburgh Daily News*.

The Grace Murder Case

One 19th century visitor wrote, "There was something extremely imposing in the profound silence with which every part of the work of these was performed."

Inmates were given a Bible to read and were allowed no visitors from the outside world. Meditation was encouraged. Some prisoners were able to memorize huge portions of the Bible. One inmate committed to memory 1,296 verses, another 1,605. Any violation of the silent system was treated with harsh and immediate punishment. Most wardens believed that to ignore any infraction committed by an inmate was to encourage rebellion. Prisons became autonomous entities, impervious to the outside world.[v]

Since food was scarce and little attention was paid to its quality, inmates were most often in a weakened condition. They received a ration of just two eggs per year and fresh fruit was extremely scarce. When some prisoners had the audacity to ask for more food, they were beaten for their efforts. The diet may explain why Bill Grace was said to have lost fifty pounds during his imprisonment. Inmates fell into a cycle of despair and despondency. Suicides were common and many prisoners simply died in their cramped, unsanitary cells. Sing Sing became symbolic of oppression and hopelessness. If a man was sent "up the river," there was a chance he was never coming back alive.[vi]

None of the newspapers mention who the executioner was, but from 1891 to 1914, Edwin Davis was the electrician at Sing Sing. Davis was the first state electrician for the State of New York and finalized many of the features of the electric chair.

This excerpt from *Agent of Death*, written by Robert Elliott, also an executioner at Sing Sing from 1926 to 1939, describes what happens when one is electrocuted. The *Newburgh Daily News*, in talking of Bill's death, says the body lurched forward,

The Execution

which is consistent with the description from a man who witnessed hundreds of electrocutions.

"The figure in the chair pitches forward, straining against the straps. There is the whining cry of the current, and a crackling, sizzling sound. The body turns a vivid red. Sparks often shoot from the electrodes. A wisp of white or dull gray smoke may rise from the top of the head or the leg on which the electrode is attached. This is produced by the drying out of the sponge, singed hair, and, despite every effort to prevent it, sometimes burning flesh. An offensive odor is generally present."[vii]

Conditions at Sing Sing were harsh. It was not until Lewis Lawes came to the prison in 1919 that things started to be transformed into a more modern penile system, so Bill Grace would have been in a tough environment.

Bill Grace was dead and life slowly returned to normal in the small Village of Walden.

The Grace Murder Case

[i] *Newburgh Daily News*, August 4, 1913, p.1
[ii] *Newburgh Daily News*, August 13, 1913, p.1
[iii] *Newburgh Daily News*, August 4, 1913, p.1
[iv] *Newburgh Daily News*, August 4, 1913, p.1
[v] Christianson, Scott. *Ossining Correctional Facility, Prisons & Prison Life*, 2001
[vi] Christianson, Scott. *Ossining Correctional Facility, Prisons & Prison Life*, 2001
[vii] Elliot, Robert, G. *Agent of Death: The Memoirs of an Executioner*, 1940, p.146

REFERENCES

Court Transcript, Court of Appeals, the People of the State of New York vs. Anthony William Grace, filed April 26, 1913.

Court Transcript, the People of the State of New York vs. Anthony William Grace, 1912.

Christianson, Scott. *Ossining Correctional Facility, Prisons & Prison Life,* NYU Press, October 2001.

Cooper, String. *Old Walden, A Condensed History of Walden and Its Early Days*, Compiled by C.E. Cooper.

Elliott, Robert G. *Agent of Death, The Memoirs of an Executioner*, NY, NY: E.P. Dutton & Co., 1940.

Sopko, Joseph. *New York Knife Company, Cultural Resources Site Examination of New York State Museum Site 10935*, The NYS Education Department, Albany, NY, 2002.

Newspapers
The Newburgh Daily News
Fall River Daily Globe
Middletown Argus
New York Times

Author Lisa Melville. Photo by James McIver

ABOUT THE AUTHOR

Lisa Melville has been an environmental planner for 20 years and has written many technical reports in this field. Currently, she is working for the New York State Department of State as their NYC Watershed Programs Coordinator. She is also a local historian and completed her Master's degree in Public History from the State University of New York at Albany in December 2005

A lifelong resident of New York State, she grew up in Walden and spent several years in Syracuse, Ithaca and Albany, New York. She is currently living in Walden with her husband and daughter.

SISU BOOKS PUBLISHING

Sisu Books is a small press located in Sparrowbush, New York. As a small press, Sisu Books proudly offers books written by regional authors in a variety of genres, including fiction, true crime, new age and history.

Sisu Books was founded in 2009 by author Michael J. Worden to provide authors in the Hudson Valley area with a quality regional press. Sisu is a Finnish word which translated to English means strength of will, tenacity, guts, mettle and courage that is sustained over time. It is the ability to overcome adversity to get the job done. Worden chose to name the small press Sisu Books largely because of a personal and strong connection he feels to this unique Finnish word.

Our library of books in print continues to expand so please visit us on the web at www.sisubooks.com or write to:

Sisu Books
PO Box 421
Sparrowbush, New York 12780

www.sisubooks.com